AMERICA'S
MORAL
COMPASS

AMERICA'S MORAL COMPASS

The Beginning of Sorrows

TINA M. RAY

Dedications

This second novel is dedicated to my Lord and Savior Jesus Christ. He is my true inspiration for authoring this book. Jesus gives us truth, knowledge, and wisdom through His Word. When I look around and see all that is going on in our world, I see the signs of the times. This book is a representation of our urgency in seeing the hourglass of our lives (sands of time) which are quickly dispersing and running out, and the direction to which America is headed, unfortunately South. Through our spiritual lenses, we see the rampant evil that is threatening our way of life. When looking at the timeline of events, God gives us warnings of things to come, things which must take place before His imminent return. While there is still time, we need to shine brighter for the cause of Christ through our testimony to the lost. America must return to the ways our forefathers paved for our great nation. There needs to be prayer, morals, and values brought back to the school system. Justice and integrity must be restored. (And the list goes on and on). Just remember, God is still on the throne and in control of all that is transpiring.

Other Dedications

First, to my church, Porter's Grove Baptist, with my pastor, Pastor Steve Dixon Jr., for the truths you are teaching, the seeds you are sowing into my life. Thank you for always being there for your congregation. Your heart to see the lost saved and added to the kingdom is the most important part of our services.

Secondly, Pastor Billy Wright of Living Waters Ministry in Summerville, Georgia. Pastor Wright has a broadcast program of weekly services and has been in the ministry for over 60 years.

Third, Pastor Mary J. Dye of Port Deposit, Md. Pastor Dye can often be found expounding on the Word and preaching the gospel at various churches, worshipping with Christian friends.

America's Moral Compass

The Beginning of Sorrow

The Lord Jesus, His thundering voice echoing through the ages, gives warnings and signs of things to come. The prophets of old have spoken His holy Word and carried out His plan for mankind. America, have you listened? Do you not fear His cup of wrath? He will judge according to His timetable. According to His Word, it is written there will be a time of Jacob's trouble. Jeremiah 30:7, "Alas! For that day is great, so that none is like it: it is even the time of Jacob's trouble, but he shall be saved out of it." During this time, the world is in total chaos; world financial systems crash into "food or famine" economic ruin. We have been experiencing higher gasoline and fuel prices, skyrocketing food prices, and businesses closing their doors resulting in massive layoffs worldwide. There is a voice crying in the wilderness, "America, we need to change." Sound familiar? No one can turn this economy around except the Lord Jesus. Church, you had better open your eyes and heed His warning. We need to pray without ceasing. The sands of time demand our immediate attention. To prepare the way, John the Baptist was the forerunner for Jesus. He cried, "Behold the lamb which taketh away the sins of the world." He spoke of the one who would save us from our sins. Jesus is the blameless, spotless lamb who was slain from the foundation of the world. He was our bondsman; we were sold on the auction block of sin, and He paid our price to set us free. No man knows the hour in which Jesus will return, no one except His Father in heaven. Look at the signs He has given us: there will be war and rumors of war, woe to them that give suck in those days, your sons and daughters will prophesy. "I will pour out my spirit in the last days." "Take the Romans' road to eternal life, follow me." "Believe on the Lord Jesus Christ in your heart and confess with your mouth that God has raised Him from the dead and ye shall be saved." America, wake up; the time of judgment is upon us, and His wrath will be the cup of judgment to judge our sin. Will ye choose this day His mercy or be condemned for eternity? The choice is up to you.

Romans 10:13, "For whosoever shall call upon the name of the Lord shall be saved."

This book is based on non-fiction and fiction. There are two symbols represented: the hourglass represents the sands of time, events still yet to come, and the compass, which shows the direction America is going (South). As we look at a worldly view and a biblical view, only one can overcome, and that is by the blood of the Lamb. The last chapter of the book, Grace Wins, will be put into action and will take place once Jesus Christ returns for His bride.

Acknowledgments

Books Read:

- *America: Imagine a World Without Her* by Dinesh D'Souza
- *Awakening* by Ralph Reed Foreword by Governor Mike Huckabee
- *Rules of War* by Matthew Betley
- The Holy Bible – King James Version

Webpages Read:

www.the bible.com

www.unitedstatesresources.com

www.WHO.org

www.newworldorder.org

www.Israelunderfire.org

www.Americajudged.org

www.cashlesssociety.org

www.antichrist.org

www.marriagesupperofthelamb.org

www.fallennation.org

www.secondcomingofChrist.org

www.raptureready.org

www.thesignofthetimes.org

News and Articles Read: FOX NEWS, CNN NEWS

Contents

Dedications v

America's Moral Compass vii

Acknowledgments ix

1. In God We Trust (Sands of Time) 1

2. United States (Richest Nation).............................7

3. 20/20 Perfect Vision.......................................19

4. Perilous Times (An Invisible Enemy) 29

5. The Winds of Change (One Voice)............................39

6. United We Stand, Divided We Fall 45

7. New World Order...51

8. Cashless Society 59

9. The War Still Rages (war and rumors of war).............65

10. Signs of the Times.......................................71

11. Beginning of Sorrow (a Time of Jacob's Trouble) 77

12. Will There Be Peace? (Israel Under Fire).................85

13. A Fallen Nation...93

14. America, Turn Back to God 103

15. God's Spirit Removed 111

16. America Judged (God's Wrath Revealed)..................125

17. Alpha and Omega, "The Beginning and End"...........135

18. A Legacy of Truth... 145

19. Truth Revealed 161

20. "Grace Wins".. 177

Bibliography/References.. 197

Chapter 1

In God We Trust (Sands of Time)

What do the sands of time represent? People have been searching for an answer to that question since time began. As we look throughout history, we can see through the scope of society's lens the lessons we have learned from our ancestors and other pioneers of faith (our innovators and teachers who have taught us about our historical background, our biblical roots, and our origin). Let us look at some examples in which the sands of time demanded our immediate attention and we did not heed the warning. We will look back at history (worldly view) and what God's Word (biblical view) has to say about it. Looking through the lens of society, we will be looking at what has happened in our nation since prayer and the Bible were taken out of school. On June 17, 1963, by an 8-1 vote, the United States Supreme Court ruled that school-sponsored Bible reading in public schools was unconstitutional. The case, Abingdon School District v. Schempp, 374 U.S. 203, removed God from public schools and profoundly altered our understanding of the separation of church and state. Below is the timeline since the 1963 Prayer in School Ruling; the debate continues over fifty years later. What has happened in the past fifty years since the ruling is astonishing and has added moral sin to our ever-changing world. (example, divorce rates are up, higher rates of suicide, teenage pregnancy is on the rise, and domestic violence is at an all-time high). A coincidence? I think not. These are products of a godless society.

- 1980 Stone v. Graham: displaying Ten Commandments in the public classroom ruled unconstitutional.

- 1983 Wallace v. Jaffra: banned "moment of silence" where students were encouraged to pray.

- 1992 Lee v. Weisman: outlawed prayers led by members of the clergy at public graduation ceremonies.

- 2000 Sante Fe Independent School District v. Doe: banned student-led prayer at public high school football games.

Children in the public-school systems are being taught secular humanism. Christian children are being taught moral relativism in direct contradiction to their faith. They are taught that people are not created in God's image but are a result of a chance mutation over millions of years. Many children are being home-schooled or sent to Christian schools.

Do we have to wonder why we are in the mess we are in? You have a lawless society, in which wrong is considered right and right is considered wrong. When we decided that we did not need prayer and Bibles in our schools, we became a product of our own making. Over the past fifty years, we have seen more and more erratic behavior. Who would have thought that before a football game, you could kneel during the national anthem or according to an official statement the NFL announced in May 2018, that it would penalize a team if its player (s) kneel during a national anthem on the field? The NFL requires that all league and team personnel stand and show respect for the flag and the anthem. Personnel who choose not to stand for the anthem are to stay in the locker room until after the national anthem has been performed. I know many who have given up watching the sport due to this very matter. Our flag still stands for freedom, but sadly, many of our God-given rights are being slowly taken away from us.

Now we are going to look at God's biblical view. A story most of us have heard at one time or the other in Sunday School, or through grandparents and other family and friends, is God's promise to never flood the earth again as He did in the days of Noah. The world was living in total wickedness; people were beating, killing, mocking, and stealing from each other. God saw the evil of men in those days and His heart was filled with pain. Noah was a good man who had a good relationship with God and found grace in the eyes of the Lord by following His commands. God told Noah to build an ark to the saving of his family: Noah, his wife, and their three sons and their wives. Noah built the ark because he believed that God would really bring the flood and really would save him. (Hebrews 11:7). Because it had never rained, many disbelieved why Noah was building an ark and mocked him for building the ark. The ark was to be built exactly as God commanded Noah, a 3-story wooden ark with rooms inside and coated with pitch. Pitch is a black, sticky waterproofing material that can be made from pine trees. The dimensions were 450 ft long, 75 ft wide, and 45 ft. high. This boat covered over ¾ of an acre. God told Noah to store on the ark every kind of food, enough for his family and two (or seven) of each kind of animal. ("Of every clean beast thou shalt take to thee by sevens, the male, and his female; and of beasts that are not clean by two, the male and his female." Genesis 7:2) Noah was told by God that his survival depended on him and his family to remain on the ark with the upcoming flood. Noah got to work following God's instructions to the letter. (Genesis 6: 17-22). When Noah completed the ark, and all were aboard (Noah and his family and two of every kind of animal) God shut them in. The Lord patiently waited until the ark was finished before bringing forth judgment on the world. (1 Peter 3: 20-21). That very day, all the springs of the great deep burst forth, and the floodgates of the heavens were opened. The rains began and ended precisely when God said they would. It rained for forty days and forty nights with fierce power. As the waters continued to rise, people were trying to get into the ark; there were frantic cries from outside the door pleading to get into the ark, but they all drowned. God wiped the slate clean by destroying every living thing not on the ark. (Genesis 6: 5-12). For 7.5 months flood waters covered the peaks of the highest mountains. Noah would send out a dove to see if there was dry land; she would return, and water remained on the land. Over a year after Noah boarded the ark, the waters finally went down, and he could step out onto dry land. He built an altar in worship of the God who had saved him, and the Lord promised never again to destroy the earth with water (Genesis 7: 1-17). God painted a rainbow across the sky, a lovely symbol of His promise. God saved Noah through God's perfect justice, not only in faithfully punishing sin but also in faithfully rescuing the few who trusted in Him. God is holy, perfect, and pure, set apart from anything sinful. Romans 3:23 says, "For all have sinned and fall short of the glory of God."

Sinful nature separates us from God because He cannot embrace wickedness. He cannot ignore sin (turn a blind eye to sin); He always does the right thing. Romans 6:23 tells us, "For the wages of sin is death; but the gift of God is eternal life through Jesus Christ our Lord."

God shows His power throughout the Bible, such as when the Lord rained burning sulfur on Sodom (a city full of arrogant, greedy women and men eager to rape anyone they could get their hands on). God spared a believer named Lot. When Lot hesitated to leave, angels grasped his hand and the hands of his wife and daughters and led them to safety, "for the Lord was merciful to them." (Genesis 19: 1-16, Ezekiel 16:49). Lot's wife turned to look back and was turned into a pillar of salt. (Genesis 19: 1526). When we do not heed God's warnings, sin always has consequences, and you should take sin and God's wrath seriously.

> Psalms 62:8. "Trust in him at all times, O people; pour out your heart before him; God is a refuge for us."

Chapter Two

United States (Richest Nation)

History gives us a glimpse of how the United States became one of the richest nations in the world. These are ten of the deep strengths that America has developed in the past that must be constantly nurtured and improved upon to continue moving in the right direction.

1. An entrepreneurial culture. The United States illustrates individuals who have desired to start businesses and grow them and are willing to accept challenges and take necessary risks. There is no penalty in the U.S. culture for failure and for starting again. (Many people have tried time and time again.) Even students who have gone to college or to a business school show this entrepreneurial desire. Facebook has inspired countless people to partake in entrepreneurial activities. Online sales have generated quite a popularity among people who take risks. The United States is known as "the land of opportunity".

2. A financial system that supports entrepreneurial activities. The United States has a more developed system of equity finance than the countries of Europe and a decentralized banking system in place that helps local entrepreneurs. The equity finance system includes "angel investors" willing to take on the task of financing the growth of firms. The national system of small local banks that provide loans to new businesses includes more than 7,000 individual small banks that are important in their local communities, providing the funds necessary to start up and run a business or businesses.

3. World-class research universities. These produce much of the basic research that is the driving force of high-tech entrepreneurial activities. Doctoral graduates and faculty members often spend much time in businesses that are located near these universities. The culture of the universities and of the businesses welcome these overlapping activities between academia and the private sector. These research universities attract talented students from all over the world, many of whom remain in the United States.

4. Labor markets that link workers and jobs unimpeded by large trade unions, state-owned enterprises, or excessively restrictive labor regulations. In the private

sector, less than seven percent of the labor force is unionized. There are no state-owned enterprises. While labor laws and regulations affect conditions and hiring rules, they are much less onerous than in Europe. ("Onerous" is defined as of a task, duty, or responsibility involving an amount of effort and difficulty that is oppressively burdensome). State-level licensing rules are probably the most serious barrier to job change and interstate mobility. In today's world, more jobs are adopting unions to settle disputes and debates.

5. A growing population, reflecting both natural growth and immigration. A growing population means a younger and therefore more flexible trainable workforce. A high degree of geographic mobility within the United States increases the effectiveness of the labor force. The higher level of real income makes the United States an attractive destination for ambitious career-driven, talented young people from around the world. Although there are restrictions in place on immigration, there are also special rules that provide access to the U.S. economy and a path for citizenship ("green cards") based on individual talent and industrial sponsorship. A separate special "green card lottery" provides a way for eager people to come into the United States.

6. A culture and tax-transfer system that encourages challenging work and long hours. On average, an ordinary employee in the United States works 1800 hours per year, longer than the 1500 hours worked in France and the 1400 hours worked in Germany. Some Asian countries, such as Hong Kong, Singapore, and Korea, work as much as 2200 hours per year.

7. A supply of energy that makes North America energy independent. The private ownership of land and mineral rights has facilitated the rapid development of fracking (the process of injecting liquid at high pressure into subterranean rocks, and boreholes, to force open existing fissures and extract oil or gas) to expand the supply of oil and gas. Up to the early 1950's, the U.S. produced most of the energy it consumed. During the mid-1950's the United States began to import greater amounts of energy, particularly crude oil, and petroleum products such as gasoline and distillate fuels to fill the gap between energy consumption and production. U.S. total energy imports increased every year until peaking in 2007. Total energy imports subsequently declined in most years through 2021 as increases in U.S. energy production offset the need for imports and contributed to increases in U.S. energy exports. (Supply and demand.) Crude oil accounts for the largest share of U.S. total energy imports on an

energy content basis. Some of the imported crude oil is refined into petroleum products that are exported. When our pipelines were shut down and thousands lost their jobs, this was an effect of the action to shut down the pipelines. According to CNN, the Keystone Pipeline shut down after an oil leak, halting 600,000 barrels a day. Do we have to wonder why gasoline prices skyrocketed?

8. A favorable regulatory environment. Although the system of government regulations needs improvement, it is less burdensome on businesses than the regulations imposed by European countries and the European Union. Restrictive measures, or sanctions, are one of the EU's tools to promote the objectives of the Common Foreign and Security Policy. These include but are not limited to safeguarding the EU's values, its fundamental interests, and security; consolidating and supporting democracy, the rule of law, human rights, and the principles of international law; preserving peace; preventing conflicts and strengthening international security.

9. A smaller size of government than in other industrial countries. The Organization for Economic Co-Operation and Development (OECD) is an intergovernmental organization with 38 member

countries founded in 1961 to stimulate economic progress and world trade. According to the OECD, outlays of the U.S. government at the federal, state, and local levels totaled 38% of GDP while the corresponding figure was 44% in Germany, 51% in Italy, and 57% in France. The higher level of government spending in other countries implies that not only is a higher share of income taken in taxes, but also that there are higher transfer payments that reduce incentives to work. So, Americans have a higher pre-tax reward for working and can keep a larger share of earnings.

10. The U.S. has a decentralized political system in which states compete. The competition among states encourages entrepreneurship and work effort and the legal systems protect the rights of property owners and entrepreneurs. The United States political system assigns many legal rules and taxing power to the fifty individual states. The states then compete for businesses and for individual residents by their legal rules and tax regimes. Some states have no income taxes and have labor laws that limit unionization. States provide high-quality universities with low tuition for in-state students. They compete also in their legal liability rules. The legal system attracts both new entrepreneurs and large corporations. The United States is unique among high-income nations in

the degree of decentralization. Question: "How do we increase the economy's growth potential?" That is a good question. Putting people back to work, lowering the costs of living, and minimizing taxes would be a good start. We need to bring God back to America, in our schools, our courthouses, our government, and repent of our sins to heal our land. One can only hope that America will return to the trend that has made it a great nation. "One Nation under God"

The keys to living a good life in the eyes of God can be found by doing the following:

Relinquishing Control

Christians like to think they have more control than they do. However, the truth is the Lord oversees our lives; He orders our steps. When we come to terms with the concept of letting go and walking the journey with Him, then living the adventure becomes easier and more enjoyable. Ephesians 2:10 states "For we are God's handiwork, recreated in Christ Jesus that we may do those good works which God predestined for us, that we may walk in them." Proverbs 10:16 says, "If you live right, the reward is a good life; if you are evil, all you have is sin." If you are going through hardship and trials, the daily grind can be taxing and detouring. Each day we must reset, connect with the Lord, and identify the things in our lives that are positive. If you are a Christian, scripture is a big part of your life. Not only does it serve as a foundation for your beliefs, but it is also a resource that you utilize for reference, reflection, and planning.

There are several ideals associated with living a good life. People hear about struggles and setbacks and oftentimes lose sight of the blessings in their own lives. In many cases, the obstacles channel strength and perseverance that we didn't know existed. Ideally, a Christian would turn to scripture and be reminded that hard times are part of life and bring forth unimaginable blessings. Generally, our culture identifies best with instant gratification; however, that is not the reality in most cases.

Living a good life requires Christians to identify goodness and positivity. Being optimistic and embracing the good with the bad will create the hope you need to survive.

Pray for Others

Not praying for others is a sin. 1 Samuel 12:23 states, "Moreover as for me, God forbid that I should sin against the Lord in ceasing to pray for you: but I will teach you the good and the right way." It is important to always look for the best in people. We are all broken and need the Great Physician to heal us. While this can be discouraging, maintaining this outlook is a way Christians can live a good life without sin.

Additionally, prayer is the main method to communicate with God. He hears our prayers and supplications. 1 Peter 3:12, "For the eyes of the Lord are over the righteous, And His ears are open unto their prayers: but the face of the Lord is against them that do evil."

Wisdom is Learned Through Obedience

Doing virtuous deeds for others and using the Lord's wisdom is instrumental to living a good fruitful life. Proverbs 3:16-17 discusses this concept. "Wisdom gives: a long, good life, riches, honor, pleasure, peace." Knowledge leads to wisdom. Proverbs 16:16, "How much better is it to get wisdom than gold! and to get understanding rather to be chosen than silver!" Proverbs 15:33 "The fear of the Lord is the instruction of wisdom; and before honor is humility." Therefore, studying scripture and assimilating the Lord's words with experiences is a crucial way Christians learn and grow in the word. Like Proverbs 19:8 says, "He that getteth wisdom loveth his own soul: he that keepeth understanding shall find good."

Get Educated on Integrity

Use scripture to create a foundational structure for your life. As individuals who have endured both good and troubled times, we assume that we know the correct way to live our lives. We set our own standards which are applicable to our own judgment versus the Bible – and ultimately what we're learning in our walk of faith. Living an integral life means abiding by the commandments and implementing those concepts and philosophies as our foundation. There are several scriptures that echo the concept of a life filled with integrity.

Deuteronomy 25:13-15 says, "Thou shalt not have in thy bag divers weights, a great and a small. Thou shalt have in thine house, divers measures, a great and a small. But thou shalt have a perfect and just weight, a perfect and just measure shalt thou have; that thy days may be lengthened in the land which the Lord thy God giveth thee."

And don't forget Proverbs 1:2, "To know wisdom and instruction; to perceive the words of understanding."

Philippians 4:8 –"Finally brethren, whatsoever things are true, whatsoever things are honest, whatsoever things are just, whatsoever things are pure, whatsoever things are lovely, whatsoever things are of a good report; if there be any virtue, and if there be any praise, think on these things."

Weigh Your Words

Do you remember hearing the old saying, "Sticks and stones may break my bones, but words will never hurt me?" This is not true; words do hurt and cut deep into the soul leaving scars that remain hurtful.

1 Peter 3:10 says, "For He that will love life, and see good days, let him refrain his tongue from evil. And the lips that they speak no guile: Let him eschew evil, and do good; Let him seek peace, and ensue it." Words are influential – they can be life-changing for good and bad. Words can bring life or death. Proverbs 18:21"Death and life are in the power of the tongue: and they that love it shall eat the fruit thereof." Ultimately, that means thinking before you speak. Proverbs 13:3 says, "He that keepeth his mouth keepeth his life: but he that openeth wide his lips shall have destruction." As a Christian and child of God, it is important to understand the weight of your words. Choose your words wisely and think about the way you would like to receive the statement you're going to make.

Making Sacrifices

Sacrifice always leads to a good life. We are taught, through scripture, to sacrifice ideals and possessions within our lives. Romans 12:1-2 –"I beseech you therefore, brethren by the mercies of God, that ye present your bodies a living sacrifice, holy, acceptable unto God, which is your reasonable service. And be not conformed to this world: but be ye transformed by the renewing of your mind, that ye may prove what is good, and acceptable, and perfect will of God." Our Father in Heaven sacrificed His Only Begotten Son to save us from our sins. Our Savior Jesus Christ carried His cross for the remission of our sins.

What is a good life, according to the gospel? Our answer embodies these six essential keys. One cannot work without the others. If a Christian breaks into one element, they must balance the others as well. No one will achieve a good life without understanding how to embrace a well-rounded mindset of all key points.

Remember your purpose and the God you serve. Understanding the full scope and maintaining an open mind will guarantee joy, prosperity, wisdom beyond your years, and fulfillment – which is a good life. And start each day by putting on the armor of God. Ephesians 6:11, "Put on the whole armor of God, that ye may be able to stand against the wiles of the devil." Ephesians 6:14-18, "Stand, therefore, having your loins girt about with truth, and having on the breastplate of righteousness; and your feet shod with the preparation of the gospel of peace; above all, taking the shield of faith, wherewith ye shall be able to quench all the fiery darts of the wicked. And take the helmet of salvation, and the sword of the spirit, (which is the word of God). Praying always with all prayer and supplication in the Spirit and watching thereunto with all perseverance and supplication for all saints."

Matthew 6:33, "But seek ye first the kingdom of God, and his righteousness; and all these things shall be added unto you."

Chapter Three

20/20 Perfect Vision

When I think back to the year 2020, I remember asking so many people what they thought 20/20 should represent. Many people reflected upon being a new upcoming year seasoned with change, others saw the year to start over with a clean slate, while others did not make comments. A friend asked if I could join her on a broadcast to speak about what I saw for the upcoming year spiritually. I was a bit nervous but saw an opportunity to speak about what I saw for my life in the upcoming year (drawing closer to my faith and starting my second novel). Time flew by and as changes occurred, that broadcast was put on the back burner for a later time. I always heard that 20/20 represented "perfect vision." If you had 20/20 eyesight, you did not have to wear contacts or have corrective lenses, you could see perfectly. The holidays were quickly approaching, and like times past, the hustle and bustle was upon us for gathering with friends and family and planning to see family and friends. This year, looking back at 2020, it seemed to be that a lot of people were sick with respiratory infections, coughing that lasted longer than a few rounds of antibiotics. This was nothing out of the ordinary, except the length of time it took to get over a respiratory infection. With flu season in full swing, many were diagnosed with pneumonia-like symptoms. Some of them were hospitalized and put on respirators while others passed away. As the winter drudged on and spring was in the next several months, a news channel broadcast a very devastating message. There was a new virus that had been discovered, and it was claiming lives at an alarming rate. Coronavirus (COVID-19) was on the horizon. Here is a timeline showing the devastating effects of COVID19, better known as the "coronavirus," according to CNN's reporting when the strange virus came on the scene.

- December 31, 2019- Cases of pneumonia detected in Wuhan, China are first reported to WHO (World Health Organization). During this reported period, the virus is unknown. The cases occur between December 12 and December 29, according to Wuhan Municipal Health.

- January 1, 2020- Chinese health authorities close the Huanan Seafood Wholesale Market after it was discovered that wild animals sold there may be the source of the virus.

- January 5, 2020- China announces that the unknown pneumonia cases in Wuhan are not SARS or MERS.

In a statement, the Wuhan Municipal Health Commission says a retrospective probe into the outbreak has been initiated.

- January 7, 2020- Chinese authorities confirm that they have identified the virus as a novel coronavirus, initially named 2019-n-Cov by WHO. Two people reportedly died between January 11 and 17, 2020, after respiratory failure caused by severe pneumonia. A 61-year-old man who was exposed to the virus at the seafood market died on January 9, 2020. On January 17, a second person died in China from the same virus and respiratory complications.

- January 17, 2020- The United States responds to the outbreak by implementing screenings for symptoms at airports in San Francisco, New York, and Los Angeles.

- January 20, 2020- China reports 139 new cases of the sickness, including a third death. On the same day, WHO's first situation report confirms cases in Japan, South Korea, and Thailand.

- January 2020- The National Institutes of Health announces that it is working on a vaccine against the coronavirus. "The NIH is in the process of taking its first steps towards the development of a vaccine," says Dr. Anthony Fauci, director of the National Institutes of Allergy and Infectious Diseases.

- January 21, 2020- Officials in Washington state confirm the first case on U.S. soil.

- January 23, 2020- At an emergency committee meeting, WHO says that the coronavirus does not constitute a public health emergency of international concern.

- January 23, 2020- According to the Beijing Culture and Tourism Bureau, to contain the growing spread of coronavirus, all large-scale Lunar New Year's celebrations were canceled.

- January 28, 2020- Chinese President Xi Jinping meets with WHO Director-General Tedros Adhanom in Beijing. At the meeting, Xi and WHO agree to send a team of international experts, including but not limited to, US Centers for Disease Control and Prevention staff, to China to investigate the coronavirus outbreak.

- January 29, 2020- The White House announces the formation of a new task force that will help monitor and contain the spread of the virus and ensure that Americans have accurate and up-to-date health and travel information.

- January 30, 2020- The United States reports its first confirmed case of person-to-person transmission of the coronavirus. On the same day, WHO determines that the outbreak constitutes a Public Health Emergency of International Concern (PHEIC).

- January 31, 2020- The Donald Trump administration announces it will deny entry to foreign nationals who have traveled in China in the last 14 days.

- February 2, 2020- A man in the Philippines dies from coronavirus, the first time a death has been reported outside mainland China since the outbreak began.

- February 3, 2020- China's Foreign Ministry accuses the US government of inappropriately reacting to the outbreak and spreading fear by enforcing travel restrictions.

- February 4, 2020- The Japanese Health Ministry announces that ten people aboard the Diamond Princess cruise ship moored in Yokohama Bay are confirmed to have coronavirus. The ship, which is carrying more than 3,700 people, is placed under quarantine scheduled to end on February 19.

- February 6, 2020- First COVID-19 death in the United States: A person in California's Santa Clara County dies of coronavirus, but the link is not confirmed until April 21.

- February 11, 2020- WHO names the coronavirus COVID-19.

- February 26, 2020- President Donald Trump places Vice President Mike Pence in charge of the US government response to the novel coronavirus, amid growing criticism of the White House's handling of the outbreak.

- March 4, 2020- The CDC (Center for Disease Control) formally removes earlier restrictions that limited coronavirus testing of the public to people in the hospital unless they had close contact with confirmed coronavirus cases. According to the CDC, clinicians should now "use their judgment to determine if a patient has signs and symptoms compatible with COVID-19 and whether the patient should be tested."

- March 11, 2020- WHO declares the novel coronavirus outbreak to be a pandemic. WHO says the outbreak is the first pandemic caused by a coronavirus. In an Oval Office address, President Trump announces that he is restricting travel from Europe to the United States for 30 days to slow the spread of coronavirus. The ban, which applies to the twenty-six countries in the Schengen Area, applies only to foreign nationals and not American citizens and permanent residents who have been screened before entering the country.

- March 13, 2020- President Trump declares a national emergency to free up $50 billion in federal resources to combat coronavirus.

- March 18, 2020- President Trump signs into law a coronavirus relief package that includes provisions for free testing for COVID-19 and paid emergency leave.

- March 19, 2020- At a news conference, officials from China's National Health Commission report no new locally transmitted coronavirus cases for the first time since the pandemic began.

- March 23, 2020- United Nations Secretary-General Antonio Guterres calls for an immediate global ceasefire amid the pandemic to fight "the common enemy."

- March 24, 2020- Japan's Prime Minister Shinzo Abe and International Olympic Committee (IOC) president Thomas Bach agree to postpone the Olympics until 2021 amid the outbreak.

- March 25, 2020- The White House and Senate leaders reach a mutual agreement on a $2 trillion stimulus deal to offset the economic damage of coronavirus, producing one of the most expensive and far-reaching measures in the history of the US Congress.

- March 27, 2020- President Trump signs the stimulus package into law.

- April 2, 2020- According to the Department of Labor, 6.6 million US workers filed for their first week of unemployment benefits in the weeks ending March 28, the highest number of initial claims in history. Globally, the total number of coronavirus cases surpasses 1 million, according to John Hopkins University's tally.

- April 3, 2020- President Trump says his administration is now recommending Americans wear "non-medical cloth" face coverings, a reversal of previous guidance that suggested masks were unnecessary for people who weren't sick.

- April 8, 2020- China reopens Wuhan after a 76-day lockdown.

- April 14, 2020- President Trump announces he is halting funding to WHO while a review is conducted, saying the review will cover WHO's "role in severely mismanaging and covering up the spread of coronavirus."

- April 28, 2020- The United States passes one million confirmed cases of the virus, according to John Hopkins.

Over the next several months into 2021, social distancing of 6 feet and wearing masks were the everyday norm. Businesses that lost revenue were forced to close their doors, resulting in worldwide layoffs. In the next chapter, I will talk about the "silent enemy" which is the pandemic.

> Psalms 111:10, "The fear of the Lord is the beginning of wisdom: A good understanding have all they that do his commandments: His praise endureth forever."

Chapter Four

Perilous Times (An Invisible Enemy)

What happened when the world stopped? People were working their jobs, living their lives, raising their children, living the American dream. People were gathered worshipping at churches and synagogues, believing in a higher power and living their lives as they saw fit. Restaurants were busily serving the public, grocery stores, pharmacies, and all other businesses were carrying on their usual busy schedules. The stock market and employment were at an all-time high. Everything seemed to be normal day-to-day living. All was at peace until an uninvited, unwelcome, silent enemy came on the scene. The media televised the unimaginable chaos that had entered our once-safe world. China and its people had contracted a virus; not just any virus, but one that came with a threat to harm the respiratory system; and with that people were suffering and dying. It was a worldwide pandemic, like nothing we had experienced before. In the next several weeks that followed, the nightmare began with all 50 states having cases. Some were hit harder than others, yet they all had the same gloomy outlook of unbelief and desperation.

(Personal protective equipment would become the norm). Our state officials would roll out new restrictions to try to stop the spread of the silent killer as days turned into weeks and weeks into months. Children would be taught at home; our schools and colleges were barren. Now our lives would be drastically changed; the essential workers would be placed strategically on the front lines saving lives; this would include doctors, nurses, surgeons, and all medical personnel. The non-essential workers would stay in their homes or work from home. Unemployment insurance would be put into action to accommodate the vast majority that would need to collect unemployment payments to make ends meet. Our large gatherings (graduations, weddings, births, funerals, and all other activities) would be reduced to a few people, forcing churches to conform to virtual online sermons and drive-through sermons. Businesses that could not keep revenue began closing their doors. Families could not attend a loved one's celebration of life or be in the hospital or nursing home as we have always done. This is the first pandemic I have experienced in my life, and I hope that it is the last. When I think about the catastrophic changes to our country since this whole pandemic entered our lives, I shudder to think that something so small, yet powerful could destroy our lives as we know it. Talk about an enemy one that is antagonistic to another, especially: one seeking to injure, overthrow, or conquer an opponent. Look at the changes we have been conditioned to make in our daily lives since the "invisible enemy" came on the scene. Retail is not the same; many large corporations took serious financial blows to their companies resulting in changes to how they conduct business. Everything is going electronic, from banking to getting important documentation. People were introduced to living a "virtual lifestyle." Schools were shut down, resulting in children relying on their own to spend time on a computer with little to no supervision. Our children suffered by not being with friends, having socialization, and having a normal social and academic life. Many failed because they did not have the structure of a routine to complete assignments. Parents who had to work outside the home were depended on their children to be self-taught. Academic scores dropped nationally. Should we be surprised? Not at all; this was not handled as it should have, and many have suffered. When school was back in session, our children had to wear masks and practice social distancing. Some of the younger kids struggled to stay in masks and this resulted in the virus being transmitted to others. If children showed any symptoms of COVID-19, they were sent home until a negative test was obtained.

Let's talk about how medicine has drastically changed, from tele-medicine to tele-counseling to virtual interviewing. With telemedicine, many medical offices and specialists went to having a video conference in reference to what ails you. Doctors could prescribe medication or send you for tests or to the hospital if needed. Hospitals were at full capacity catering to the severe and chronic COVID-19 cases. Many people needed surgeries that were postponed until a later time. Several businesses put shields in their offices and professional buildings to create a barrier between themselves and you. There was a season of taking temperatures before you could be seen by a doctor or other businesses or even at your job. As of the writing of this book, masks are still worn in most government buildings and medical facilities.

Now we will look at the timeline timeline of important dates that have shaped how we live and how we continue to fight the invisible enemy, from testing facilities to where we are almost three years later and compare notes. This ugly intruder has not gone away; it is still creeping around. The symptoms may be milder, but still, it is a part of our communities. We now look at it as another virus such as the flu that has infiltrated our world. (We now are a little wiser to its devices and know how to treat it.)

- May 4, 2020- During a virtual pledging conference co-hosted by the European Union, world leaders pledge a total of $8 billion for the development and deployment of diagnostics, treatments, and vaccines against novel coronavirus.

- May 11, 2020- President Trump and his administration announce that the federal government is sending

$11 billion to states to expand coronavirus testing capabilities. The relief package signed on April 24 includes $25 billion for testing, with $11 billion for states, localities, territories, and tribes.

- May 27, 2020- Data collected by Johns Hopkins University reports that the coronavirus has killed more than 100,000 people across the U.S., meaning that an average of almost 900 Americans died each day since the first known coronavirus-related death was reported nearly four months earlier.

- June 2, 2020- Wuhan's Health Commission announces that it has completed coronavirus tests on 9.9 million of its residents with no new cases found.

- June 11, 2020- According to Johns Hopkins, the United States passes 2 million confirmed cases of the virus.

- July 6, 2020- In an open letter published in the Journal of Clinical Infectious Diseases, 239 scientists from around the world urge WHO and other health agencies to be more forthright in explaining the potential airborne transmission of coronavirus. In the letter, scientists write that "studies have demonstrated beyond any reasonable doubt that viruses are released during exhalation, talking, and coughing in microdroplets small enough to remain aloft in the air and pose a risk of exposure at distances beyond 1 to 2 meters (yards) from an infected individual."

- July 7, 2020- The Trump administration notifies Congress and the United Nations that the United States is formally withdrawing from WHO. The withdrawal goes into effect on July 6, 2021.

- July 27, 2020- A vaccine being developed by the Vaccine Research Center at the National Institutes of Health's National Institute of Allergy and Infectious Diseases, in partnership with the biotechnology company, Moderna enters Phase 3 testing. The trial is expected to enroll about 30,000 adult volunteers and evaluate the safety of the vaccine and whether it can prevent symptomatic COVID-19 after two doses, among other outcomes.

- August 23, 2020- The FDA issues an emergency use authorization for the use of convalescent plasma to treat COVID-19. It is made using the blood of people who have recovered from coronavirus infections.

- August 27, 2020- The CDC notifies public health officials around the United States to prepare to distribute a potential coronavirus vaccine as soon as late October. In the documents, posted by The New York Times, the CDC provides planning scenarios to help states prepare and advise on who should get vaccinated first: health care professionals, essential workers, national security "populations," and longterm care facility residents and staff.

- December 10, 2020- Vaccine advisers to the FDA vote to recommend the agency grant emergency use authorization to Pfizer and BioNTech's coronavirus vaccine.

- December 14, 2020- U.S. officials announce the first doses of the FDA-authorized Pfizer vaccine have been delivered to all 50 states, the District of Columbia, and Puerto Rico.

- December 18, 2020- The FDA authorizes a second coronavirus vaccine made by Moderna for emergency use. "The emergency use authorization allows the vaccine to be distributed in the U.S. for use in individuals 18 years and older," the FDA said in a tweet.

- January 20, 2021- Newly elected U.S. President Joe Biden halts the United States' withdrawal from WHO.

- February 22, 2021- The death toll from COVID-19 exceeds 500,000 in the United States.

- February 27, 2021- The FDA grants emergency use authorization to Johnson & Johnson's Covid-19 vaccine, the first single-dose COVID-19 vaccine available in the U.S.

- April 17, 2021- The global tally of deaths from COVID-19 surpasses 3 million, according to data collected by John Hopkins.

As this virus continues to populate our world, there have been other "variants" of the virus such as the delta variant, which according to the CDC accounts for an estimated 93.4% of coronavirus circulating in the United States during the last two weeks of July.

- August 23, 2021- The FDA grants full approval to the Pfizer/BioNTech COVID-19 vaccine for people aged 16 and older, making it the first coronavirus vaccine approved by the FDA.

- September 24, 2020- CDC Director Dr. Rochelle Walensky diverges from the agency's independent vaccine advisers to recommend boosters for a broader group of people, those ages 18-64 who are at increased risk of COVID-19 because of their workplaces or institutional settings, in addition to older adults, long-term care facility residents, and some people with underlying health conditions.

- November 2, 2021- CDC Director Rochelle Walensky says she is endorsing a recommendation to vaccinate children ages 5-11 against COVID-19, clearing the way for immediate vaccination of the youngest age group yet in the U.S.

- November 19, 2021- The FDA authorizes boosters of the Pfizer/BioNTech and Moderna Covid-19 vaccines for all adults. On the same day, the CDC endorsed boosters for all adults.

- December 16, 2021- The CDC changes its recommendations for COVID-19 vaccines to make clear that shots made by Moderna and Pfizer/BioNTech are preferred over Johnson & Johnson's vaccine.

- December 22, 2021- The FDA authorizes Pfizer's antiviral pill, Paxlovid, to treat COVID-19. This is the first antiviral COVID-19 pill authorized in the United States for ill people to take at home before they become sick enough to be hospitalized.

- December 27, 2021- The CDC shortens the recommended times that people should isolate when they've tested positive for COVID-19 from 10 days to five days if they don't have symptoms and if they wear a mask around others for at least five more days. The CDC also shortens the recommended time for people to quarantine if they are exposed to the virus to a similar five days if they are vaccinated.

- January 31, 2022- The FDA grants full approval to Moderna's Covid-19 vaccine for those ages 18 and older. This is the second Coronavirus vaccine given full approval by the FDA.

Since there have been other booster shots people can take, I honestly have lost count of how many boosters were recommended. As this virus continues to be in our world and remains a threat, and more people contact the dreaded respiratory sickness, it is always sensible to err on the side of caution and get checked out through local pharmacies and or testing at home or by seeing your primary physician. Research and do what best works for you for the best possible outcome and a healthier you.

My personal belief that all these things are happening is because we are reaping what we have sown in this morally corrupt world. If people would repent and turn back to God, He would heal our land.

> Luke 21:11, "And great earthquakes shall be
> in divers places, and famines, and pestilences;
> and fearful sights and great signs there shall
> be from heaven."

Chapter Five

The Winds of Change (One Voice)

What is the voice we hear in the distance? Sounds like we were promised good change, but that didn't happen, looking at a timeline since our last presidential election. (Politically speaking.) Unemployment is at an all-time high, and even though there seems to be a barrage of jobs, people aren't eager to work, which has resulted in longer wait times at restaurants, grocery stores, and other businesses. Food prices have skyrocketed (have you seen the prices of eggs?), I guess chickens are on strike, gasoline prices are unaffordable for most families, and some people are just getting by. Does that sound like a change we needed? "Absolutely not." Things are always shifting; however, if the cost of living continues to rise, we will be entering a great depression/recession. Remember, history has a way of repeating itself. Looking through the lens of history, the Great Depression varied substantially across countries. The Depression was particularly long and severe in the United States and Europe; it was milder in Japan and much of Latin America. This, the worst depression ever experienced by the world economy, stemmed from a multitude of causes. Declines in consumer demand, financial panics, and misguided government policies caused the economy to suffer economic output decline in the United States, while the gold standard, which linked nearly all the countries of the world in a network of fixed currency exchange rates, played a key role in transmitting the American downturn to other countries. Recovery from the Great Depression was spurred largely by the abandonment of the gold standard and the ensuing monetary expansion. The economic impact of the Great Depression was enormous, including, but not limited to, both extreme human suffering and profound changes in economic policy. In the summer of 1929, the Great Depression began in the United States as an ordinary recession. The downturn became remarkably worse; real output and prices fell very quickly. Between the peak and the trough of the downturn, industrial production in the United States declined 47 percent and real gross domestic product also (GDP) fell. The wholesale price index declined 33 percent (such declines in the price level are referred to as deflation). The unemployment rate exceeded 20 percent at its highest point. One of the causes of the decline was a reduction in spending (sometimes referred to as aggregate demand), which led to a curtailment of production as manufacturers and merchandisers noticed an unintended rise in inventories. The next event that took place was Black Thursday, better known as the stock market crash. Stock prices had risen more than fourfold from the low in 1921 to the peak in 1929. A likely explanation is that the financial crisis generated considerable uncertainty about future income, which in turn led consumers and firms to put off purchases of durable goods; this contributed to falling production and employment in the United States. Another reason for the rapid decline of American wealth was banking panics and monetary contraction. In the fall of 1930, when the first of four waves of banking panic gripped the United States, a banking panic arose when many depositors no longer trusted or lost confidence in the solvency of banks and demanded that their bank deposits be paid in cash. Banks must liquidate loans to raise the required cash. The panics took a severe toll on the American banking system. By 1933, one-fifth of the banks in existence at the start of 1930 had failed. Let's discuss misguided government policies. Many historians believe that state governments failed to deal with the magnitude of the Depression by (1) diminishing tax revenues, (2) constitutional/statutory debt restrictions, such as balanced budget requirements, (3) localism, (4) outdated administrative organizations, and (5) inefficient and weak political leadership.

When we look at today's economy and our financial future, does it seem doom and gloom? As things continue to get out of hand and inflation continues to rise, it will become more like the Great Depression/recession. Now let us investigate God's Word and see with a biblical lens how we are to get through this time in history. First and foremost, we must trust God and put our times, passions, desires, goals, and dreams in His hands. Psalms 31:15, "My times are in thy hand: deliver me from the hand of my enemies, and from them that persecute me." The key is to know His name. Know who He is and what He promises. He promises He will never forsake you, ever. He will never leave you, and He promises that He will always provide for you. Proverbs 3:5-6, "Trust in the Lord with all thine heart; and lean not unto thine own understanding. In all thy ways acknowledge him, and he shall direct thy paths." It is a childlike confidence in our Heavenly Father. We learn to acknowledge Him every day in everything, and He promises that He will direct our lives.

The battlefield of life is our minds; we must constantly monitor our thoughts and feelings. We must refuse negative thought patterns and refuse to allow our minds to sink into thoughts of anxiety, worry, unworthiness, and hopelessness. We must be guardians of what we think. Proverbs 23:7, "For as he thinketh in his heart, so is he: Eat and drink, saith he to thee; but his heart is not with thee." Trusting God begins with our thoughts. Romans 12:2, "And be not conformed to this world: but be ye transformed by the renewing of your mind, that ye may prove what is that good, and acceptable, and perfect, will of God." Next, we must saturate our minds and hearts with the Word of God. Daily reading of God's Word is such an important part of our learning to trust God. Matthew 4:4, "But he answered and said, It is written, Man shall not live by bread alone, but by every word that proceedeth out of the mouth of God." Just as we need physical food for survival, we need spiritual food to fulfill us and sustain us spiritually. The Bible is the word of life; it gives light; it gives wisdom. It reveals to us the heart of God. 2 Timothy 3:16-17, "All scripture is given by inspiration of God, and is profitable for doctrine, for reproof, for correction, for instruction in righteousness: That the man of God may be perfect, thoroughly furnished unto all good works." And finally, we should replace negative thoughts and feelings with the promises of God. There are thousands of promises printed in the Bible concerning life, relationships, and the circumstances we face each day. Each promise is built upon the faithfulness and steadfast love of God. It is impossible for God to lie. Hebrews 6:18, "That by two immutable things, in which it was impossible for God to lie, we might have a strong consolation, who have fled for refuge to lay hold upon the hope set before us."

> 2 Timothy 3:1-5, "This know also, that in the last days, perilous times shall come. For men shall be lovers of their own selves, covetous, boasters, proud, blasphemers, disobedient to parents, unthankful, unholy. Without natural affection, trucebreakers, false accusers, incontinent, fierce, despisers of those that are good. Traitors, heady, high-minded, lovers of pleasures more than lovers of God; Having a form of godliness but denying the power thereof; from such turn away."

Chapter Six

United We Stand, Divided We Fall

History has shown us how we are united; one brotherhood/sisterhood was what made us a strong nation. The laws of the land, our constitutional rights, and our God-given rights are slowly diminishing. Things in our history that once stood for a free country have vanished, and since then things in our world have been replaced by a secular worldly agenda aimed at getting our eyes off the truth, swaying our constitutional rights, and setting the stage for a oneworld government. Many of our traditional figures are off the map now because of so-called racist theory, such as Aunt Jemima Syrup being replaced with Pearl Milling Co., Uncle Ben Rice with Ben's Original and the list goes on and on. The United States of America was known as the great melting pot. There are all races that have contributed to the greatness of our nation.

Dr. Martin Luther King Jr. was a Baptist minister who became the predominant leader in the civil rights movement to end racial segregation and discrimination in America during the 1950s and 1960s; he was a leading spokesperson for nonviolent methods of achieving social change. His eloquence as a speaker and his personal charisma— combined with his deeply rooted determination to establish equality among all races despite personal risk – won him a worldwide following. Dr. Martin Luther King Jr. had a great message; he wanted to live in a world where everyone was valued. Dr. King held many rallies to unite people. Dr. King advocated for nonviolence, education, and love as the means to achieve social change, and challenged his followers to "be the change that you wish to see in the world." Another famous quote of Dr. King was "Darkness cannot drive out darkness: only light can do that. Hate cannot drive out hate: only love can do that." See *Martin Luther King Jr., a Testament of Hope: The Essential Writings and Speeches.*

In the 21st century, there are many leaders who are shaping America. I choose to talk about visionary Howard Schultz, the founder and CEO of Starbucks, who has exhibited resilience and creativity in guiding his company through many challenges. One of the golden threads of his leadership is a relentless focus on the customer experience. From product offerings to details such as the shape of its tables, Starbucks strives to serve the customer, taking the customer's point of view. To accomplish that, Schultz created an exemplary relationship with Starbucks employees. The company's financial success also demonstrates that a commitment to diversity can be a competitive edge in attracting talent in the 21st century. In a reflection of the breaking of traditional boundaries, Schultz also entered the political arena with a book expressing his vision. Though his steps into national electoral politics did not bear fruit, he will surely remain in the arena.

We will now look at seven facts that prove America is in deep trouble, why the return is so critical, and conclude what steps are needed to move forward one nation under God.

1. When Ronald Reagan won his first election, the U.S. national debt was less than $1 trillion. When Barack Obama came into the White House, the debt sat at $10.6 trillion; when Republicans took control of the House of Representatives in 2010, it was about $14 trillion, and now we have reached the $25 trillion mark and climbing due to COVID-19 aid. Americans don't seem to care that we are rapidly bankrupting our nation.

2. In 1956, approximately 5% of all babies in the United States were born to unmarried mothers. Today, things have obviously changed tremendously; 2008 was the very first year in United States history when 40% of all babies were born to unmarried mothers.

3. In the early 1970s, well over 60% of all Americans were "middle class," but in 2015 that number had more than doubled.

4. In 2001, nearly 16 million Americans could not afford the homes that they were living in, but by 2015 that number had more than doubled.

5. Our system of public education is a complete mess. A study of millennials in 22 major industrialized nations conducted by the Educational Testing Service found that only two countries were worse than the U.S. when it came to literacy proficiency, and the U.S. was dead last in math.

6   In the early 1970s, 70% of all men in the United States between 20 and 39 were married, but today that number has fallen to just 35%. Instead of getting married and starting families, many young men are still living at home with their parents. Today, 35 % of all young men between 21 and 30 "are living at home with their parents or a close relative."

7. Many Americans don't realize this, but the United States has the highest rate of illegal drug use on the entire planet. But we have an even bigger problem with legal drugs. According to a study conducted by the Mayo Clinic, nearly 70% of all Americans are on at least five prescription drugs.

What must we do to come back to a rightful stand? Are we the generation that will witness the end of America?

Throughout human history, every great society has eventually entered a period of decline, and sadly we are experiencing the same demise as well. Our prayer should be that our nation will return to the values and principles upon which this nation was founded. The course that America and much of the world are on depends on the upcoming election, the shaking of the virus, and the need for world revival.

"'Return to me, and I will return to you,' says the Lord of hosts." – Malachi 3:7

We are in a crucial period; the sands of time are demanding our full attention, and we have been warned. God in His mercy has afforded us a time of reprieve to turn and repent for our land to be spared from destruction. It's a Nineveh moment. Remember the story of Jonah who ran from the presence of the Lord and was on a ship going to Tarshish? God sent a great wind into the sea, and there was a mighty tempest so that the ship was like to be broken. The shipmaster came unto Jonah, who had fallen asleep, and told him to call upon his God, so they wouldn't perish sea then became calm, and Jonah was swallowed by a great fish; he was in the belly of the fish for three days and three nights. When Jonah was spared and spewed out of the mouth of the great fish onto dry land, he then repented and went to Nineveh as God had commanded him. Jonah was to go to Nineveh and cry against it, for their wickedness had come up before God.

Joel 2:12-13 states "There also now, saith the Lord, turn ye even to me with all your heart, and with fasting, and with weeping, and with mourning: And rend your heart, and not your garments, and turn unto the Lord your God: for he is gracious and merciful, slow to anger and of great kindness, and repenteth him of the evil."

Return to the Lord your God, for He is gracious and merciful, slow to anger, and abounding in steadfast love, and He relents over disaster. Without revival, America and its future will be lost. Therefore, we have a window of time we may never have again. Most of us don't want to look at the negative, but a few positive glimmers here and there give a false sense of security to what is really happening in our nation.

> Psalms 138:7, "Though I walk in the midst of trouble, thou wilt revive me: Thou shalt stretch forth thine hand against the wrath of mine enemies, and thy right hand shall save me."

Chapter Seven

New World Order

When we look at current world events, we see them setting the stage behind the scenes. A conspiracy theory comes to mind, a world in which there is the genuine prospect of a new world order. In the words of Winston Churchill, "a world order in which the principles of justice and fair play protect the weak against the strong." "A world where the United Nations, freed from Cold War stalemate, is poised to fulfill the historic vision of its founders." "A world in which freedom and respect for human rights find a home among all nations." The New World Order is a term used to define the period of dramatic change in the world of politics. Although the term has been interpreted differently, it is basically related to the idea of global governance, particularly in the aspect of a collective effort to identify, diagnose, and tackle worldwide challenges that an individual nation or state cannot handle on its own. People are becoming politically active, politically aware, and politically interactive. Global activism against oppression and the need for cultural respect and economic freedom is gaining momentum worldwide. Nations are real.

The well-known use of the term "new world order" was in connection with the Fourteen Points by Woodrow Wilson after World War I and during the creation of the League of Nations. World War I highlighted the need to create a safer world for democracy. Wilson proposed a new world order which was to transcend the usual great power politics. He emphasized the need to collectively enhance security, democracy, and self-determination. However, Americans refused to be part of the League of Nations, which Wilson viewed as key to the new world order. The term was also used sparingly after World War II, during the creation of the United Nations. It fell from use partly because of the failure of the League of Nations, while others perceived it as a projection of the American dream.

The term "new world order" as used during the post-Cold War era had no definite meaning. It may have been redefined progressively in three different periods: by the Soviets, the US before the Malta Conference, and after September 11, 1990. Initially, the new world order dealt exclusively with nuclear disarmament but was later expanded by Gorbachev to include the strengthening of the UN, utilizing the need to fight a common enemy together rather than individually. The phrase has been in use since its inception, especially in the political field. In 1994, Henry Kissinger claimed that a new world order was not possible without the US participation since it was the most significant component. Former UK Prime Minister Tony Blair used the phrase in November 2000 and in 2001 to

2003 while calling for a new world order. Another former UK Prime Minister, Gordon Brown, also called for a new world order in 2008 while on a tour to New Delhi. He also used the phrase at the G20 Summit forum comprising 19 countries and the European Union (EU). It worked to address major issues in 2009 in London. (A summit is an intergovernmental meeting, to discuss topics such as international financial stability, climate change, and sustainable development.)

Several other world leaders such as Mahmoud Ahmadinejad, the Iranian President, and his Georgian counterpart, Mikheil Saakashvili, have also called for a new world order. Some scholars have also advanced their thesis on the declining global influence of the US and the rising of illiberal powers, including China. Political analysts such as Leonid Grinin of Russia acknowledge the US will continue to play a critical role in the new world order. Keys to power are reserve currencies that are commonly accepted around the world, so having one is key to a country becoming rich and powerful. All countries or empires that stood at the top of the world order at any given time knew and did this. A new world order begins with a new dominant power and the establishment of a world monetary system. Therefore, you see, it is not about greedy bankers and politicians. They are just cogs in the wheel of order, playing a part that would be insignificant if they stood alone. But nothing that runs a system ever works alone. At the core there are two things that cause a shift in world order; it comes down to countries spending more than they make, and internal conflicts of the country.

The following are stages that go from the rise to the decline of any given world order

1. War

2. Peace and growing prosperity

3. Financial bubble

4. Reserve currency

5. Wealth gap

6. Financial bubble bursts

7. Printing money

8. Revolution for wealth distribution

9. Diminishing power relative to external rivals

10. External conflicts

11. New winners

12. Winners create the new world order

13. Back to step one

When we speak of war, a new world order begins when revolutionary new orders go to war and defeat weak and old orders. Peace and growing prosperity are when victory in war gets the winners together and the dominant power establishes orders, such as monetary systems, that will work for them. (This period of peace also favors growth and prosperity). When we speak of the financial bubble, as people grow and prosper, they begin taking on debt to get further ahead in life (such as keeping up with the Joneses). This begins a financial bubble as people begin spending much more than they earn and begin racking up credit card debt and other avenues of borrowing money. It is true that in some cases, as most people make more money and become wealthier, they abandon the idea of working. Worse yet, their offspring are raised in luxury, mellowed by wealth, and unfit for much of the work. (We are seeing this in our society today.)

Reserve currency- the New World Order has the currency of the dominant power as the reserve currency. This also makes that country's ability to borrow much higher than other countries with no reserve currency. (Therefore, countries end up increasing their spending too far, outmatching their incomes.) All the money being pumped into the country causes money to flow to the top and remain concentrated in the hands of those with businesses or investments, creating a wealth gap. (This gap between the "haves and have-nots" continues to increase as the country keeps pumping more money into the system.) Soon all this spending more than the country makes comes to a point where the country cannot pay back its debts and the financial bubble bursts. (Sound familiar? It's happening to people in the United States). The central bank then prints money to pay back its debts. (As more money enters the market without an increase in the country's productivity, it goes into buying things such as stocks, gold, and other existing commodities.) This causes the prices of those things to increase as the value of the currency drops.

Revolution for wealth distribution- this is when the increase in prices further widens the wealth gap to the point that conflicts arise. (People begin fighting each other based on status and values.) All this bickering and the fight for scarce resources leaves the country less productive, thereby leading to many weaknesses such as diminishing shares in the global market which will cause diminishing power relative to external rivals. Then we will see external conflicts; if the loss of power continues, there is another country that is on the rise. This country soon reaches a point where it can take on and challenge the bigger country. These conflicts lead to war, and since the old country is already weakened by internal conflict, it may lose the war, leading to new winners. New winners create a New World Order (sit in agreements as dominant powers and establish a new world monetary system including but not limited to changing the reserve currency).

In conclusion, based on how diverse the countries' cultures are, and how big the world is, it would be naïve to think that any one country can ever create a one-world government. America is not yet to the point where the shifts are inescapable, but it's getting close. Let us view what God's Word has to say about this very topic. **Revelation 21: 1-3**, "And I saw a new heaven and a new earth: for the first heaven and the first earth were passed away; and there was no more sea. And I John saw the holy city, new Jerusalem, coming down from God out of heaven, prepared as a bride adorned for her husband. And I heard a great voice out of heaven saying, Behold the tabernacle of God is with men, and he will dwell with them, and they shall be his people, and God himself shall be with them, and be their God." Revelation 21: 21-25, "And the twelve gates were twelve pearls; every several gate was of one pearl: and the street of the city was pure gold, as it were transparent glass. And I saw no temple therein: for the Lord God Almighty and the Lamb are the temple of it. And the city had no need of the sun, neither of the moon, to shine in it: and the kings of the earth do bring their glory and honor into it. And the nations of them which are saved shall walk in the light of it: and the kings of the earth do bring their glory and honor into it. And the gates of it shall not shut at all by day: for there shall be no night there."

Revelations 13: 16-18, "And he causeth all, both small and great, rich, and poor, free and bond, to receive a mark in their right hand or in their foreheads: And that no man might buy or sell, save he that had the mark, or the name of the beast, or the number of his name. Here is wisdom, Let him that hath understanding count the number of the beast: for it is the number of man; and his number is Six hundred threescore and six."

Chapter Eight

Cashless Society

After COVID-19 came on the scene, many people did not want to touch money; everything was being sanitized (people did not want to touch anything that someone else touched). What is one of the dirtiest, most germ-infested things that easily passes from one person's hand to the other? You guessed it, it is the almighty dollar, our currency (cold hard cash and coins). Businesses did not take long to decide that they did not want cashiers managing cash from every random customer coming in from off the street. They started pushing for cashless payments, the use of only cards to cut back on the spread of germs. There were signs posted on the windows and doors stating, "not accepting cash" and "cards only." This was popping up all over the country. Somehow cards were germ-proof or safer to use than cash. Dollar bills and currency have always had a grime on them, as they are cycled daily by banks, businesses, and customers. During this time of pandemic, the great American coin shortage happened. When businesses were closed, there was no exchange of coins; therefore, the U.S. Mint had fewer staff members on hand to produce the sum of coins it normally produced. Cash is still king; it is easier to spend more when you swipe a card than to give cash for your purchases.

Some people use virtual mobile wallets and just swipe away like they are playing virtual Monopoly. Before you wipe away your savings, make sure what you take out to spend is budgeted in your banking account. You need to plan for every expense so that you can make the most of your money. Proponents (the other side of the coin) of a cashless society argue that digital transactions are more convenient for both the customer and businesses and that a cashless society would cut down on many criminal activities. There are potential drawbacks to a cashless society: first, it excludes a large part of society who are "unbanked" (mostly poor) persons who do not use or cannot obtain a bank account. Second, it could invite serious breaches of privacy, because few purchases and sales would be anonymous. Third, even minor technological glitches could block access to funds, and systematic failures due to natural disasters or massive hacking could make all purchases and payments impossible. Fourth, during a severe economic crisis threatening the solvency of major banks, depositors would be unable to access their funds (rescue their money by withdrawing it in cash).

This is a lot to think about before changing our historical currency to virtual everything. Let us look at the pros and cons of a cashless society.

Advantages of digital currency.

1. *Faster transactions* – The transaction is made in an instant, offering individuals a lot more time. No one likes standing in line for groceries while people search for cash and count it. Simply paying with their card would be more practical. (Digital payments facilitated the rise of online stores; it made shopping more straightforward, with a lot of filters and sorting options.)

2. *Better financial management* - Having your bank account linked to a digital wallet gives users access to their financial inputs and outputs history, and offers a better view of spending habits.

3. *More security against scams and thieves* - Credit or debit cards can be blocked with a single call to bank support. If your phone gets stolen, you can always use someone else's phone to call. A financial history is also an excellent backup for fraud. (Ex., online vendors that never delivered your order, online courses that never took place mixed up orders, you have the evidence that this was paid, along with the exact time of payment).

4. *Digital money is clean* - Cash is continuously moving around from hand to hand. Digital money is a cleaner option.

Disadvantages of digital currency.

1. *Low literacy rate* - This is one of the top causes for multiple existing issues. People who live in underprivileged areas of the world without access to electricity and water such as India rely entirely on cash. Therefore, there are no computers or internet available.

2. *Chances of corruption* - one cannot guarantee crime will not be generated due to hackers. A person exercising a bribe in money might necessitate it in kind instead of cash.

3. *Economic disparity* - If the standard payment technique gets changed into a cashless system completely, the chances of purchasing smartphones or devices will be necessary. In a country such as India, this would be considered a luxury; many citizens endeavor to provide for their daily food and necessities and could not afford such a luxury.

4. *Overspending* - There is no doubting the truth that cashless transactions are more straightforward than simply making a mere click; people can execute payments. The advantage of transactions leads to an overspending tendency, particularly among the modern generation. This will lead to more debts that cannot be paid back and further plunge people into debt.

5. *Identity fraud* - The risk of identity fraud is one of the most significant disadvantages of a digital currency cashless society/economy in the world. The rate of online fraud is growing and continues to prove the perils of hacking. Not every person is tech-savvy and exceptionally aware of all the usage of technological gadgets. While attempting to make digital transactions, many people might end up disseminating their personal identity in the online forum of creepy lurkers/hackers.

What does God's Word say about our currency? Let us understand God's Word on this difficult subject.

> We know since the currency was first minted;
> we have "In God We Trust."

> I Timothy 6:10 – "For the love of money is the root of all evil: which while some coveted after, they have erred from the faith, and pierced themselves through with many sorrows."

> Deuteronomy 15:6"For the Lord thy God blesseth thee, as he promised thee: and thou shalt lend unto many nations, but thou shalt not borrow; and thou shalt reign over many nations, but they shall not reign over thee."

Ecclesiastes 5:19"Every man also to whom God hath given riches and wealth, and hath given him power to eat thereof, and to take his portion, and to rejoice in his labor; this is the gift of God."

Matthew 6:24 "No man can serve two masters: for either he will hate the one and love the other; or else he will hold to the one and despise the other. Ye cannot serve God and mammon."

Matthew 6:21"For where your treasure is, there will your heart be also."

2 Timothy 3: 1-5 –"This know also, that in the last days perilous times shall come. For men shall be lovers of their own selves, covetous, boasters, proud, blasphemers, disobedient to parents, unthankful, unholy, without natural affection, truce breakers, false accusers, incontinent, fierce, despisers of those that are good, Traitors, heady, high-minded, lovers of pleasures more than lovers of God; Having a form of godliness but denying the power thereof; from such turn away".

Chapter 9

The War Still Rages (war and rumors of war)

The battle cry is at the door. Let truth march on; we must endure. We are in a spiritual battle, people; this is not a fantasy or fairytale. We are soldiers in the army of God. And as good soldiers, we must prepare for the battlefield. In the last days, there will be war and rumors of war. People's hearts will wax cold against the truth; many will fall away from their faith. Let us look through the scope of what is happening in our world to indicate that we are on the verge of preparing for a great war. (God have mercy in our time of trouble.)

The U.S. faces both the immediacy of Great Power competition and the prospect of Great Power war. Both require a military that is completely prepared for combat. This preparation includes all the customary aspects of military power — personnel, material, and training. But the most important and least measurable is *intellectual* readiness. Being prepared by having a strategic mindset plan of action is most important in defeating the enemy.

A military organization's first peacetime task is preparing for combat. Americans could be forgiven for forgetting this fact, given the state of our contemporary political debate, some of which has drawn the military into the political dispute. This political tension combines with recent American combat experience to further conceal the military's true purpose. These conflicts demand officers who take the initiative, operate without extensive support, are extremely skillful in small-unit tactics, and are comfortable working with local political actors. Some of these skills translate to Great Power warfare, but most are practiced at the lower levels of command. This is especially true of naval and air officers. At no point since Vietnam have they been asked to wage a long-term air-control campaign, and at no point since 1945 have they been required to secure sea control against a capable adversary.

The United States' entire national style is defined by the application of overwhelming material superiority against an adversary. Exceptions exist — for example, Grant and Sherman's operational brilliance late in the Civil War — but in general, major American wars follow an identical pattern: an initial defensive period during which the U.S. mobilizes resources, followed by a punishing counterattack that overwhelms the adversary.

The key, again, is *material* superiority, which in today's U.S. military amounts to a scant faith that technology and industrial capacity can prevail against foes with greater initial military competence. But there is no end in sight to China's arms buildup. China is increasing in military power and supplies. The U.S. ought to consider the possibility that China will possess larger forces than ours, and we should look upon the exceptional military competence of Israel as a model. Underscoring this is the U.S.'s vastly diminished ability to equal American industry's extraordinary World War II output. The U.S. may not have its former ability to overcome a powerful enemy with material in time to prevail.

The U.S. military today is focused on budget battles, sourcing issues, social engineering, and the permanent quest of large central military staff to increase their hold on everything from strategy to force architecture. As important as these are, they distract from warfighting. The understanding that the U.S. is in an interwar period does not exist. The notion that the military's first task is to defeat our increasingly powerful adversaries is a remnant of the unexamined past. The results of our military's inability to imagine, plan, and exercise accordingly to deter or defeat China are more readily apparent. Since we know that the hourglass is shifting the sands of time, we must also prepare for the war that will take place in the last days: the Battle of Armageddon. Armageddon- this refers to great destruction and disaster, either a physical event such as a natural disaster or a spiritual event, such as the end of the world. The word "Armageddon" originated from the Hebrew word "Har Megiddo" which means "mountain of Megiddo." This term is used in the Bible to signify the final apocalyptic battle between God's armies and demonic beings; that will be the final confrontation between good and evil. The battle of Armageddon is mentioned in the book of Revelation; the battle will take place on the plains of Megiddo in Israel, and it will be the climax of all the previous battles that have taken place between God and Satan.

Revelations 16: 21 says, "…and there fell upon men a great hail out of heaven, every stone about the weight of a talent; and men blasphemed God because of the plague of the hail: for the plague thereof was exceeding great."

What will happen at the end of the world? The end of civilization. In this battle, the armies of the Antichrist are challenged by God's chosen people, the Jews. In the world, the Antichrist is the embodiment of all evil. God will triumph over the antichrist and defeat him.

Rise of the Antichrist

Three and a half years into the seven-year tribulation period, the antichrist places what Jesus called the Abomination of Desolation in the Holy Place in the temple of Jerusalem. This is a small statue of the Antichrist which comes alive and desecrates the place of sacrifice. Mark 13:14,. "But when you see the abomination of desolation, spoken of by

Daniel the prophet, standing where it ought not, (let him that readeth understand) then let them that be in Judaea flee to the mountains."

The Abomination of Desolation compels Jews to worship the Antichrist. This is crucial to his plan to attain a world dictatorship. The Antichrist demands to be worshipped and brands all his followers with 666. John tells us in 1 John 2:22, "Who is a liar but he that denieth that Jesus is the Christ? He is the antichrist, that denies the Father and the Son." Many will take the number 666 to avoid economic sanctions but be doomed to eternal damnation in hell. Those who refuse to take the number and will not follow or worship the Antichrist will be put to death as martyrs. Satan is in full control and personally indwells the Antichrist in the last three and a half years of the tribulation.

In the Bible, Ezekiel's Vision of the Valley of Dry Bones.

Ezekiel 37: 1-10, "The hand of the Lord was upon me, and carried me out, and set me in the midst of the valley was full of bones. And caused me to pass by them round about: and behold, there were very many in about: and behold there were very many in the open valley: and, lo, they were very dry. And he said unto me, Son of man, can these bones live? And I answered, O Lord God, thou knowest. Again, he said unto me, Prophesy upon these bones, and say unto them, O ye dry bones hear the word of the Lord. Thou saith the Lord God unto these bones; Behold, I will cause breath to enter you, and ye shall live. And I will lay sinews upon you and will bring up flesh upon you, and cover you with skin, and put breath in you, and ye shall live, and ye shall know that I am the Lord. So, I prophesized as I was commanded, there was a noise, and behold a shaking, and the bones came together, bone to his bone. And when I beheld, lo, the sinews and the flesh came upon them, and the skin covered them above; but there was no breath in them. Then said he unto me, Prophesy unto the wind, prophesy son of man, and say to the wind, thus saith the Lord God; Come from the four winds, O breath, and breathe upon these slain, that they may live. So, I prophesized as he commanded me, and the breath came into them, and they lived, and stood upon their feet, an exceeding great army."

The vision of dry bones coming together to make up a skeleton being covered with flesh and coming back to life is a prediction of the Jewish people coming together from places all over the world to become a living, breathing soul. In 1948 this became a reality, with Jews all over the world returning to Israel and establishing a nation.

Psalms 27:5, "For in the time of trouble he shall hide me in his pavilion: In the secret of his tabernacle shall he hide me; he shall set me upon a rock."

Chapter Ten

Signs of the Times

When we look at what is currently happening in our world, it seems as if at any given moment we could hear the trumpet sound. All who are in the body of Christ await the blessed moment, when in the twinkling of an eye, we shall be changed. Jesus will split the eastern sky and return for His bride, the dead in Christ shall rise and meet Him in the air. And all the redeemed shall meet Him in the air. Time as we know it will vanish as if a vapor, and God's judgment will be accomplished.

As we reflect and ponder all of eternity, where do you want to spend eternity? I hope you will choose the streets of gold, not the weeping, wailing, and gnashing of teeth, in an eternal burning hell, to be eternally separated from your Creator.

Jesus's will is for all to come to repentance, be saved, and live eternally with our Creator in heaven forever. Jesus died for the remission of our sins.

Let us view some of the events that are happening in our ever-changing world. Looking at California (the Golden State) they are currently dealing with a deadly bomb cyclone weather pattern that has produced flooding rain, debris flows, damaging winds, and massive waves that have dissipated off the West Coast, but there are additional atmospheric river storms that will continue throughout the next several days. According to Fox Forecast Center, there is scant hope for drier weather in California anytime soon.

The next round of heavier rain is forecasted to move into the coastal ranges of Northern California and Southern Oregon, courtesy of another atmospheric river. Rainfall could quickly become hazardous and lead to scattered instances of flash flooding. The consistent stream of moisture being funneled out of the tropical Pacific Ocean will cause more damage to surrounding areas. On the higher elevations of the Sierra Nevada mountain range, Northern California will see more rounds of heavy snow.

The weather patterns have been catastrophic in many areas of the world. Some blame it on global warming, but I say it is up to our Creator, not Mother Nature.

Next, we will look at Israel and what is happening in that part of our world. Israel is under attack in the middle of a crossfire.

According to Fox News recently in YEHUD, Israel – It was a night of terror for people from Jerusalem to Gaza, including people not necessarily involved in politics who had no way of knowing who would be safe, who might be spared.

When Hamas delivered an ultimatum to the Israelis to stop their strikes on high-rise buildings at 9 p.m. Tuesday, Israel ignored it.

Hamas made good on its threat to hit the heart of Israel, sending rockets raining on Tel Aviv, yet another serious escalation in this hot conflict. Dozens of rockets headed toward Israel's most vibrant city. Three people in neighboring communities were killed. Two of them, a father, and his daughter, happened to be Arab.

"We heard a huge 'boom' over our head. The whole shelter shook like crazy. My partner said 'OK, the house is gone,'" he recounted. He said he felt very lucky to be alive. If it hadn't been for the bomb shelter in his house, he wouldn't be. If he hadn't run when the sirens went off, following well-known instructions here, he and his family probably wouldn't have been around to tell their story. "The shelter was filled with dust, smoke," he said. "We opened the door, and the basement was filled with dust. We could not see anything. "Israel Defense Forces spokesman Jonathan Conricus said this onslaught by Hamas has been more ferocious this time.

"Unfortunately, Hamas, under international support, I'd say, has been able to stockpile weapons into the Gaza Strip and also to manufacture weapons by themselves homemade inside Gaza using a lot of financial aid from Iran and Iranian knowledge," Conricus said. "They've invested heavily. They've got trained people. They have facilities, technology, the minds, and brains to do that," he told Fox News. "Hamas and the Islamists — they were the first to rely on new media and the internet. They do not have to go through borders so they can be checked and searched. It is easy to check email and you've got instructions. "The volume and intensity of Hamas rocket attacks has been a new twist to an old and violent act. But so has this. The Arab youth of Israel — those living not in the Palestinian territories but within Israel — has started rising in frustration. "It's the inequalities, the unequal rule for Palestinians versus the Jewish population. It is nonsense," explained Chehab, who said the world will be hearing plenty more from the young generation of Arabs living in Israel.

There have been numerous demonstrations that have spiraled into violence with provocation on both sides — not a development the Israeli government is welcoming, and it is not clear where it will end. Enemies have always gone against Israel and God has always protected them as His chosen people. Jews are going back to their homeland; this is prophesized in the Bible. We will revisit Israel under fire in a subsequent chapter.

Let us view God's Word to know how we are to live while awaiting His second coming. 2 Timothy 2:15, "Study to shew thyself approved unto God, a workman that needeth not to be ashamed, rightly dividing the word of truth."

> Matthew 28: 18-20, "Go ye therefore, and teach all nations, baptizing them in the name of the Father, and of the Son, and of the Holy Ghost: Teaching them to observe all things whatsoever I have commanded you: and, lo, I am with you always, even unto the end of the world, Amen."

> Luke 21:36, "Watch ye therefore, and pray always, that ye may be accounted worthy to escape all these things that shall come to pass, and to stand before the Son of man."

> Matthew 24:7, "For nations shall rise against nation, and kingdom against kingdom: and there shall be famines, and pestilences, and earthquakes in divers places."

> The definition of divers places just means many or varied.

> Luke 21:11, "And great earthquakes shall be in divers places, and famines, and pestilences; and fearful sights and great signs shall there be from heaven."

God has given us specific commandments to follow as we follow Him in love.

> Joel 2:28, "And it shall come to pass afterward, that I will pour out my spirit upon all flesh; and your sons and daughters shall prophesy, your old men shall dream dreams, your young men shall see visions."

Chapter 11

Beginning of Sorrow
(a Time of Jacob's Trouble)

The Bible speaks of a time in which the world is in utter chaos. It is a time never seen before in our history. What does it mean "there will be famine in the land?" To better explain this, famine means severe and prolonged hunger in a substantial proportion of the population of a region or country, resulting in widespread and acute malnutrition, and death by starvation and disease. In our world today, we have already experienced a lack of supplies and high demand for our daily essentials such as not enough food or supplies for our daily living. We experienced a lack of formula for our children and medication shortages, just to name a few. We have seen the workforce dwindle and businesses shut down. Our workforce is not what it used to be; unemployment is at an all-time high. This has continued as a trend since the midpoint of 2020. We have seen ships that were stuck out in the ocean with merchandise and materials, resulting in major delays, due to a lack of employees and manpower. One company that has remained on top is Amazon, which will deliver overnight or the next day. There have been so many changes we have undergone since our world took a major turn or downfall. "Nothing is the same; medical offices, professional offices, banks, and all other businesses run differently." "This is the beginning of sorrow." In the Old Testament, God foretold an unparalleled time of trouble, characterized by birth pangs but followed by the return of scattered Jews to their homeland to serve the Lord and live in peace under a Davidic king (Jeremiah 30: 4-10).

The phrase "the time of Jacob's trouble" comes from Jeremiah 30:7, which says "Alas! For that day is great, so that none is like it: it is even the time of Jacob's trouble; but he shall be saved out of it." In the previous verses of Jeremiah 30, the Lord is speaking to Jeremiah the prophet about Judah and Israel (Jeremiah 30: 3-6). In verse 3, the Lord promises that one day in the future, He will bring both Judah and Israel back to the land He had promised their forefathers. But their return will involve many distresses: "How awful that day will be! It will be the time of Jacob's trouble- Jacob being an advocate for all the nation of Israel." Verse 5 describes Jacob's trouble as a time of great fear and trembling. "For thus saith the Lord, we have heard a voice of trembling, of fear and not of peace." Verse 6 describes it in terms of the pains of childbirth, indicating a time of agony. But there is hope for the people of Israel, for the Lord promises He will save them. Even though this is the time of Jacob's distress and even though "in all of history there has never been such a time of terror," God will deliver His people. Like Jeremiah,

Jesus described the tribulation as a unique time of suffering, speaking of "great distress, unequaled from the beginning of the world until now and never to be equated again." (Matthew 24:21). Matthew 24: 6-8 states, "And you will hear of wars and rumors of wars, see that you are not troubled; for all these things must come to pass, but the end is not yet. For nation will rise against nation and kingdom against kingdom." The Lord also used some of the same imagery as Jeremiah. He said the appearance of false Christs, wars and rumors of war, famines and earthquakes are "the beginning of birth pains." Paul described the tribulation in 1 Thessalonians 5:3 says, "while people are saying, 'peace and safety,' destruction will come on them suddenly, as labor pains on a pregnant woman, and they will not escape." The time of Jacob's trouble demonstrates that God is faithful in keeping His promises, judging sin, and saving those who trust in Christ.

As the time of Christ's return draws near, Satan will direct his wrath not only toward faithful Christians but toward the physical descendants of all Israel.

Shortly after the return of Christ, all the descendants of ancient Israel—including the descendants of the so-called lost ten tribes—will again gather and resettle in Palestine. Jerusalem will once more be the capital of the restored Twelve Tribes of Israel, as well as the capital of the world.

This reunion of all twelve tribes is described in some detail in Ezekiel 37: 15-28, which says, "The word of the Lord came again to me, saying, Moreover, thou son of man, take thee one stick, and write upon it, For Judah and the children of Israel his companions: And join them one to another into one stick, and they shall become one in thine hand. And the children of thy people shall speak unto thee, saying, Wilt thou not shew us what thou meanest by these? Say unto them, Thus saith the Lord God; Behold, I will take the stick of Joseph, which is in the hand of Ephraim, and the tribes of Israel his fellows, and will put them with him, even with the stick of Judah, and make them one stick, and they shall be one in mine hand. And the sticks thereon thou writest shall be in thine hand before their eyes. And shall thou say unto them, Thus saith the Lord God; Behold I will take the children of Israel from among the heathen, whither they be gone, and I will gather them on every side, and bring them into their own land. And I will make them one nation in the land upon the mountains of Israel, and one king shall be king to them all, and they shall be no more two nations, neither shall they be divided into two kingdoms anymore at all. Neither shall they defile themselves anymore with their idols, nor with their detestable things, nor with any of their transgressors: but I will save them out of all their dwelling places, wherein they have sinned, and will cleanse them: so, shall they be my people, and I will be their God. And David my servant shall be king over them, and they shall have one shepherd: they shall also walk in my judgments, and observe my statutes, and do them. And they shall dwell in the land that I have given unto Jacob my servant, wherein your fathers have dwelt; and they shall dwell therein, even they, and their children, and their children's children forever: and my servant David shall be their prince forever. Moreover, I will make a covenant of peace with them; it shall be an everlasting covenant with them: and I will place them and multiply them: and will set my sanctuary in the midst of them for evermore. My tabernacle also shall be with them: yea, I will be their God, and they shall be my people. And the heathen shall know that I the Lord do sanctify Israel when my sanctuary shall be in the midst of them forevermore."

> Jeremiah 30:3, "For, lo, the days come, saith the Lord, that I will bring again the captivity of my people Israel and Judah, saith the Lord: and I will cause them to return to the land that I gave to their fathers, and they shall possess it."

God also indicated to Jeremiah that, while He would allow the future descendants of the ancient kingdoms of Israel and Judah to fall into captivity, He would also rescue some of them from it.

He calls this end-time catastrophe—especially on the descendants of ancient Israel's northern kingdom, now known only as the lost ten tribes—the time of Jacob's trouble.

God revealed to Daniel that such a time of trouble would occur at the time of the end: Daniel 12: 1 says, "At that time Michael shall stand up, the great prince who standeth for the children of thy people: and there shall be a time of trouble."

This and other prophecies indicate that Satan's wrath during the last days will be directed not only toward faithful Christians but also toward the ethnic descendants of all of Israel—the Jews as well as the descendants of the lost ten tribes whose identity Satan has never forgotten.

It will be especially directed toward the United States, Britain, Canada, and the other British-descended peoples who are the modern-day descendants of Joseph's sons Ephraim and Manasseh.

Notice the reassurances God gives to all the long-suffering people of Israel in the last days:

"'So then, the days are coming,' declares the Lord, 'when people will no longer say, 'As surely as the Lord lives, who brought the Israelites up out of Egypt,' but they will say, Therefore, behold, the days come, saith the Lord, that they shall no more say, The Lord liveth, which brought up the children of Israel out of the land of Egypt; But the Lord liveth, which brought up and which led the seed of the house of Israel out of the north country, and from all countries whither

I had driven them; and they shall dwell in their own land." (Jeremiah 23: 7-8)

"'Therefore, fear thou not, O my servant Jacob,' saith the Lord; 'neither be dismayed, O Israel: for lo, I will save thee from afar, and thy seed from the land of their captivity; and Jacob shall return, and shall be in rest, and be quiet, and none shall make him afraid.

"'Behold I will bring them from the north country, and gather them from the coasts of the earth, and with them the blind and lame, the woman with child together; a great company shall return thither. They shall come with weeping, and with supplications will I lead them: I will cause them to walk by the rivers of waters in a straight way, wherein they shall not stumble for I am a father to Israel, and Ephraim is my firstborn.'" (Jeremiah 31: 8-9)

Once Christ rescues the ethnic descendants of ancient Israel from this "time of Jacob's trouble" in the last days, He will use them to fulfill the role their forefathers agreed to carry out in the time of Moses. He will make them the world's model people, a nation of teachers, a kingdom of priests. "And ye shall be unto me a kingdom of priests and a holy nation. These are the words which thou shall speak unto the children of Israel." (Exodus 19:6) (Compare Deuteronomy 4: 5-8 and Zechariah 8:23). "Behold I have taught you statutes and judgments, even as the Lord my God commanded me, that ye should do so in the land whither ye go to possess it. Keep therefore and do them; for this is your wisdom and your understanding in the sight of the nations, which shall hear all these statutes, and say, surely this great nation is wise and understanding people. For what nation is there so great, who hath God so nigh unto them, as the Lord our God is in all things that we call upon Him for. And what nation is there so great, that hath statutes and judgments so righteous as all this law, which I set before you this day. Thus, saith the Lord of hosts; In those days it shall come to pass, that ten men shall take hold out of all languages of the nations, even shall take hold of the skirt of him that is a Jew, saying, we will go with you: for we have heard that God is with you. (Zechariah 8:23)

> Jeremiah 30:23, "Behold, the whirlwind of the Lord goeth forth with fury, a continuing whirlwind: it shall fall with pain upon the head of the wicked."

Chapter Twelve

Will There Be Peace? (Israel Under Fire)

We will now look at the land, the history, and the people of Israel. It is at the top of the world. It is about the size of New Jersey; it is a small country in the Middle East. It is located on the eastern shores of the Mediterranean Sea and is bordered by Jordan, Lebanon, Egypt, and Syria. Israel has many important archaeological and religious sites considered sacred by Jews, Muslims, and Christians alike, and a complex history with periods of peace and conflict. *The Land of Israel.*

In the Bible, we read about Israel. Genesis 12:5"And Abram took Sarai his wife, and Lot his brother's son, and all their substance that they had gathered, and the souls that they had gotten in Haran; and they went forth to go into the land of Canaan; and into the land of Canaan they came." Shortly after Abraham and Sarah came to Canaan, a famine forced them to leave for Egypt. Scripture describes this trip as a "descent." The sages note that Israel is metaphorically higher than all the other lands, making travel to Israel an ascent and leaving it a descent. Those who returned to Israel in the time of Ezra and Nehemiah are referred to as the Olei Bavel (ascenders from

Babylon) and in modern dialect moving to Israel is referred to as Aliyah (ascent).

Early History of Israel.

Much of what scholars know about Israel's ancient history comes from the Hebrew Bible. According to the text, Israel's origins can be traced back to Abraham, who is the father of both Judaism (through his son Isaac) and Islam (through his son Ishmael). Abraham's descendants were thought to have been enslaved by the Egyptians for hundreds of years before settling in Canaan, which is approximately the region of modern-day Israel. The word Israel comes from Abraham's grandson, Jacob, who was renamed "Israel" by God in the bible.

King David and King Solomon.

King David ruled the region around 1000 B.C. His son, who became King Solomon, is credited with building the first temple in ancient Jerusalem. In about 931 B.C., the area was divided into two kingdoms: Israel in the north and Judah in the south. Around 722 B.C., the Assyrians invaded and destroyed the northern kingdom of Israel. The first temple was destroyed in 586 BC by Nebuchadnezzar, the king of Babylon when he conquered Jerusalem. The second temple was built in 586 BC after the return of Jews to Jerusalem from their exile in Babylon in 538 BC. It was destroyed in 70 AD.

Conflict between Jews and Arabs.

Throughout Israel's extensive history, tensions between Jews and Arab Muslims have continued to cause war against one another. The complex hostility between the two dates all the way back to ancient times when they both populated the area and deemed it holy. Both Jews and Muslims consider the city of Jerusalem sacred; it contains the Temple Mount, which includes the holy sites of al-Aqsa Mosque, the Western Wall, the Dome of the Rock, and more. Much of the conflict in recent years has centered around who is occupying the following areas:

West Bank: A territory that divides part of modern-day Israel and Jordan.

Golan Heights: A rocky plateau located between Syria and modern-day Israel.

Gaza Strip: A piece of land located between Egypt and modern-day Israel.

The Zionism Movement.

In the late 19th and early 20th century, an organized religious and political movement known as Zionism emerged among Jews. Zionists wanted to reestablish a Jewish homeland in Palestine. Massive numbers of Jews immigrated to the ancient holy land and built settlements. Between 1882 and 1903, about 35,000 Jews relocated to Palestine. Another 40,000 settled in the area between 1904 and 1914. Many Jews living in Europe and elsewhere, fearing persecution during the Nazi reign, found refuge in Palestine and embraced Zionism. After the Holocaust and World War II ended, members of the Zionist movement primarily focused on creating an independent Jewish state. Arabs in Palestine resisted Zionism, and tensions between the two groups continued. An Arab nationalist movement developed as a result.

Israeli Independence.

The United Nations approved a plan to partition Palestine into Jewish and Arab states in 1947, but it was rejected by the Arabs. In May 1948, Israel was officially declared an independent state with David Ben-Gurion, the head of the Jewish Agency, as the prime minister. While this historic event seemed to be a victory for Jews, it also marked the beginning of more violence with the Arabs.

Israel Today.

Clashes between Israelis and Palestinians are still commonplace. Key territories of land are divided, but some are claimed by both groups. For instance, they both cite Jerusalem as their capital. Both groups blame each other for terror attacks that kill civilians. While Israel does not officially recognize Palestine as a state, more than 135 UN member nations do.

The Two-State Solution.

Several countries have pushed for more peace agreements in recent years. Many have suggested a two-state solution but acknowledge that Israelis and Palestinians are unlikely to settle on the borders. Israeli Prime Minister Benjamin Netanyahu has supported the two-state solution but has felt pressure to change his stance. The United States is one of Israel's closest allies. In May 2017, President Donald Trump visited Israel to encourage Prime Minister Benjamin Netanyahu to embrace peace agreements with Palestinians. In May 2018, the U.S. Embassy relocated from Tel Aviv to Jerusalem, which Palestinians perceived as a signal of American support for Jerusalem as Israel's capital. Palestinians responded with protests at the Gaza-Israel border, which were met with Israeli force resulting in the deaths of dozens of protesters. While Israel has been plagued by unpredictable war and violence in the past, many national leaders and citizens are hoping for a secure, stable nation in the future. According to foreign policy news, President Donald J. Trump brokered a historic peace agreement between Israel and Sudan. President Trump, since taking office, worked to rebuild trust with our regional partners and identify their shared interests, moving them away from the conflicts of the past. Thanks to President Trump's leadership in creating the conditions for peace, the Middle East and Africa are experiencing the most rapid geopolitical transformation in over a generation. As more countries normalize relations with Israel, the region will become more stable, secure, and prosperous. The United States will continue to stand with the people of the region as they work to rebuild a brighter, more hopeful future. They are choosing a future in which Arabs, Israelis, Muslims, Jews, and Christians can live together, pray together, and dream together, side by side, in harmony, community, and peace. God made a covenant with His people Israel to make them a great nation. He would also send a Savior to rescue Israel from oppression. That Savior ushered in a new religion: Christianity. Israel was no longer the sole recipient of God's grace and care, yet Israel is still important to a full understanding of God and the Christian faith.

The Importance of Israel.

God had chosen Israel "for his treasured possession, out of all the peoples who are on the face of the earth," Deuteronomy 14:2. We must get to know His beloved people for these five reasons: their interactions with God reveal His character. The Bible demonstrates and displays God's mercy, righteousness, consistency, reliability, wrath, love, goodness, and His almighty power towards the nation of Israel. Through this relationship, God created evidence by which skeptics could test His omniscience, omnipotence, and goodness. Jesus emerged from Israel. He told His prophets that God would come down, and He would be an Israelite whose lineage could be traced back directly through the great patriarchs. Christ connected Israel with the New Church. Finally, by their pattern of sin and redemption, Israel plays out in the gospel and foreshadows the coming of Christ.

Israel and the Character of God.

Zephaniah 3 says a lot about the Lord's formidable anger, justice, and jealousy. He told His people what He wanted from them, but they disobeyed. He said, "Surely you will fear me; you will accept correction." They did not, so the Lord promised "to gather nations, to assemble kingdoms, to pour out upon them my indignation, all my burning anger; for in the fire of my jealousy all the earth shall be consumed." His wrath would not burn forever, though; later verses look forward to a time of relief, speaking of that day in the past tense as a reality in which Israel could place their trust. "The Lord has taken away judgments against you; he has cleared away your enemies. The King of Israel, the Lord, is in your midst; you shall never again fear evil." We as Christians should give reverence and trust that God means what He says. Through obedience, He will make a way of mercy and grace.

> Proverbs 9:10, "The fear of the Lord is the beginning of wisdom: and the knowledge of the holy is understanding."

Chapter Thirteen

A Fallen Nation

What would America look like without her liberties? The Statue of Liberty stands for freedom. She sits in the harbor with her torch, a symbol of all that she represents. The Statue of Liberty is an icon, a national treasure, and one of the most recognizable figures in the world. Each year millions who cherish her ideals make the journey to experience her history and grandeur in person. She is the Statue of Liberty, a symbol representing freedom, inspiration, and hope. It is recognized as a symbol for the United States of America; show the image of the statue to anyone from the Far East, Europe, or Australia and they will readily recognize that it stands for the United States. For over 145 years, the Statue of Liberty has stood tall, beckoning to countless multitudes of people who have come to her shores. According to national archives history, here are a few facts about our national treasure.

1. As American as the Liberty Statue is, it was not even an American who designed her or inspired her shape and form.

2. The real name for the Statue of Liberty is Liberty Enlightening the World. However, she has come to be known and referred to as Lady Liberty. She is the oldest statue in the United States, surpassing the Abraham Lincoln statue by 34 years.

3. The Statue of Liberty may appear as if she is standing still but her right foot is in mid-stride, which means she is moving forward. This is meant to represent her leading the way towards freedom.

4. The statue was designed by Frederic Auguste Bartholdi, a French sculptor. Bartholdi tried to pitch a similar structure to another country, but the deal fell through. A few design tweaks later, what would become the Statue of Liberty was presented to the United States to commemorate the centennial of the independence of the United States and celebrate the country's friendship with Bartholdi's native France. The U.S. and France were allies during the Revolutionary War.

5. The statue is the product of crowdsourcing. According to Google source, crowdsourcing is the practice of obtaining information or input into a task or project by enlisting the services of many people, either paid or unpaid, typically via the Internet. "Organizations are increasingly turning to volunteers to spark

innovation through crowdsourcing." Although the statue was paid for by the French government, its pedestal needed funding. Efforts to raise money were largely unsuccessful and even the American Congress could not come up with a sufficient funding package. Thanks to the efforts of Joseph Pulitzer, the famed publisher of The New York World, a fundraising campaign helped to complete the amount needed to pay for the statue's pedestal.

6. The statue has a crown with seven points, which represents the seven continents and the seven seas. It may also represent the seven different freedoms: moral, civil, national, natural, personal, political, and religious.

7. The crown is accessible to the public. There are tickets to the crown that can be bought from Statue Cruises or authorized third parties. However, people must usually book in advance due to the popularity of the tour. On non-busy days, it may be possible to gain an entry ticket simply by showing up, but this is not recommended for busy days.

How did America get to the place it is in history as a fallen nation? As our liberties are being slowly taken away from us, we are losing the battle for freedom of speech, the freedom to bear arms, and our God-given rights in religion. Let us look at the rise and fall of the United States from a biblical perspective.

The United States had its beginning when thirteen colonies declared their independence and defeated the British army. Citizens have enjoyed liberty from its humble beginning. This liberty led to prosperity, which led to the United States becoming the most powerful nation in the world. However, the United States is still just "a speck of dust on the scales" of Almighty God. Isaiah 40:15"Behold, the nations are like a drop from the bucket and are counted as the small dust of the balance. Behold, He taketh up the isles as a very little thing." Currently, this country seems to be in decline-morally, economically, and in terms of personal liberty. Here are some questions to ask yourselves:

1. Does the United States hold a special place in God's plan for mankind?

2. Has God blessed the United States because of its founding upon biblical principles? (We are a Christian nation of believers; there are still many people to be reached for the cause of Christ).

3. Is the United States in danger of divine punishment for the growing tolerance of immoral sins such as abortion and homosexuality? Let us examine what God has to say about these questions, His ultimate plan and purpose.

God's Use of Nations in Biblical Times.

The book of Isaiah indicates God is far above every nation that has existed or will ever exist. The nations that God used in the Old Testament had one thing in common-they were used in a way that related to the coming of Christ Jesus. In Genesis 46:2-3 we read, "And God spake unto Israel in the visions of the night, and said Jacob, Jacob, and he said, Here am I. And He said I am God, the God of thy father: fear not to go down into Egypt; for I will there make of thee a great nation." Egypt would provide the place for the children of Israel to grow into "a great nation." The nation of Israel itself was established and the lineage preserved so that the promise of Christ could be fulfilled. Deuteronomy 7: 7-8 says, "The Lord did not set His love upon you, nor choose you because you were more in number than any people; for ye were the fewest of all people: but because the Lord loved you, and because He would keep the oath which He had sworn unto your fathers, hath the Lord brought you out with a mighty hand, and redeemed you out of the house of the bondsmen, from the hand of Pharaoh king of Egypt." In Daniel 4:25 Nebuchadnezzar was told "That they shall drive thee from men, and thy dwelling shall be with the beasts of the field, and they shall make thee to eat grass as oxen, and they shall wet thee with the dew of heaven, and seven times shall pass over thee, till thou know that the most high ruleth in the kingdom of men, and giveth it to whomsoever will." The

Highest is ruler over the realm of mankind and bestows it on whomever He wishes. Nebuchadnezzar's nation, Babylon, had a specific place in God's plan. Nebuchadnezzar's dream is in Daniel 2: 3135. "Thou, O king, sawest and behold a great image. This great image, whose brightness was excellent, stood before thee; and the form thereof was terrible. This image's head was of fine gold, his breast and his arms of silver, his belly and his thighs of brass, His legs of iron, his feet part of iron and part of clay. Thou sawest till that a stone was cut out without hands, which smote the image upon his feet that were of iron and clay and break them to pieces" Then was the iron, the clay, the brass, the silver, and the gold, broken to pieces together, and became like the chaff of the summer threshing floors; and the wind carried them away, that no place was found for them: and the stone that smote the image became a great mountain, and filled the whole earth." The kingdoms referred to in Nebuchadnezzar's dream, the Babylonian, Medo-Persian, Greek and Roman empires, were all leading to the "fullness of time." Galatians 4:4-7, "But when the fullness of time was come, God sent forth His Son, made of a woman, made under the law, to redeem them that were under the law, that we might receive the adoption of sons. And because ye are sons, God hath sent forth the Spirit of His Son into your hearts, crying, Abba Father. Wherefore thou are no more a servant, but a son, and if a son, then an heir of God through Christ."

God's Purpose for the United States (And other Nations).

Scriptures teach that God has a purpose-a divinely ordained role for every nation. God will punish evildoers and protect the innocent. Romans 13:3-4, "For rulers are not a terror to good works, but to the evil, Wilt thou not be afraid of the power? Do that which is good, and thou shalt have praise of the same. For he is a minister of God to thee for good. But if thou do that which is evil, be afraid; for he beareth not the sword in vain: for he is the minister of God, a revenger to execute wrath upon him that doeth evil." 1 Timothy 2:2 states, "For kings and for all that are in authority; that we may lead a quiet and peaceable life in all godliness and honesty." They are to provide and maintain a free environment so that we may lead a tranquil and quiet life in all godliness and dignity. Every government including the government of the United States has this as their divine purpose.

Sin: Consequences and Divine Punishment.

As our government forsakes its divinely appointed purpose and society becomes more immoral, America will be judged for allowing that immorality. God has punished nations, not just individuals, for sin through wars, economic hardship, pestilence, captivities, and other catastrophic events. Without divine revelation, we cannot confidently affirm divine action being persuaded to give up sin by obeying the truth in John

8: 32-34, which states, "And ye shall know the truth, and the truth shall make you free. They answered him, We be Abraham's seed, and were never in bondage to any man: how sayest thou, ye shall be made free? Jesus answered them, Verily, verily I say unto you, whosoever committeth sin is a servant of sin."

Sometimes Tragedies Just Happen.

Jesus spoke of two tragedies: one caused deliberately by man, and one caused by an accident. In both cases, there would have been a tendency for men to attribute some divine action to the tragedy as a punishment for sin. Yet Jesus told them not to jump to such a conclusion. As a wise man wrote, "Time and chance overtake them all." Ecclesiastes 9:11 states "I returned, and saw under the sun, that the race is not to the swift, nor the battle to the strong, neither yet bread to the wise, nor yet riches to men of understanding, nor yet favour to men of skill; but time and chance happeneth to them all."

There is Another Punishment for Sin.

We can affirm by faith that sin often has negative consequences that come with it. Solomon said, in Proverbs 13:15, "Good understanding giveth favour: but the way of transgressors is hard." As the people of our nation become more tolerant toward and engaged in the practice of various sins (abortion, divorce for any cause, homosexuality, slothfulness) and compromising biblical principles, there will be negative consequences. The death that comes as a punishment for sin is not a physical death, but a spiritual death, eternal separation from God for eternity. Romans 6:23 states, "For the wages of sin is death; but the gift of God is eternal life through Jesus Christ our Lord." We are seeing many of these consequences of sinful behavior in our generation. Without a change in people, these sins and their consequences will only get worse.

Scripture teaches us that there are certain things about which we must try to persuade people to believe the gospel, for it is "the power of God for salvation." Romans 1:16, "For I am not ashamed of the gospel of Christ: for it is the power of God unto salvation to every one that believeth: to the Jew first, and also to the Greek." Persuade them to give up sin by obeying the truth. If everyone was obedient to the Word of God, civil government would not even be necessary. Romans 13: 8-10 states, "Owe no man anything, but to love one another: for he that loveth another hath fulfilled the law. For this, Thou shalt not commit adultery, Thou shalt not kill, Thou shalt not steal, Thou shalt not bear false witness, Thou shalt not covet; and if there be any other commandments, it is briefly comprehended in this saying, namely, Thou shalt love thy neighbor as thyself. Love worketh no ill to his neighbor: therefore, love is the fulfilling of the law." Persuade them to put their faith in God, not in man. The psalmist wrote, "It is better to trust in the Lord than to put confidence in man. It is better to trust in the Lord than to put confidence in princes. All nations compassed me about: but in the name of the Lord will I destroy them." God's chosen nation is the church and all that make up the bride of Christ. In writing to Christians, Peter said, "But ye are a chosen generation, a royal priesthood, an holy nation, a peculiar people; they ye shall show forth the praises of Him who has called you, out of darkness into His marvelous light." (1 Peter 2:9).

> Matthew 6:33, "But seek ye first the kingdom of God and His righteousness: and all these things shall be added unto you."

Chapter Fourteen

America, Turn Back to God

In a world of sorrow, we see events unfolding before our very eyes; sin running rampant, we see so much death and destruction in our world today. We have forgotten where our humble roots were planted. We have forgotten what our constitutional rights represent: freedom, prosperity, and liberty. America has forgotten that God has blessed her and continues to bless our country through His marvelous grace and mercy. However, sin cannot continue to rule our land; there is a day of reckoning what is right and holy. The only hope we have is in Jesus. What will happen if America doesn't get back on the right track? The only thing that can happen is sin will only become more accepted in society, and we will lose future generations. Our children and grandchildren and their children will live in a lawless society and continue down the wrong path. This only leads to the destruction and moral decay of our society.

The Loss of a Moral Compass Spreads.

What begins in the home will eventually spread to the community, the government, and our nation. Judges, 17:6

says, "In those days there was no king in Israel, but every man did that which was right in his own eyes." We see a nation that had lost its moral compass; every man did what he wanted to. The eventual result was God's judgment on the nation. It always seems to happen in the same order: moral decay at home, then the community, then the church, and then the government. Then when God brings judgement, people wonder what's happening. Then as chaos is happening, we are left with bigger problems in society. A spiritual clean-up is needed in the hearts of the people. 2 Chronicles 7:14 says, "If my people, which are called by my name, shall humble themselves, and pray, and seek my face, and turn from their wicked ways; then will I hear from heaven, and will forgive their sin, and will heal their land."

We live in dark, perilous times. When we turn on our televisions and our computers each day, we see young men and women violently killed by police and cops assassinated on the streets, we see crime and destruction in our cities as people commit hideous crimes. Ordinary events such as natural disasters and earthquakes report heavy losses of life. Political candidates are not trusted to carry out their oaths in office and have created social division. Peace and unity have become foreign terms. There is no question that there is a great deal at stake. Given our nation's state of turmoil, many people have wondered and questioned if God's wrath has already fallen on America. Are we beginning to enter the end times? What will

America's future be? The Bible addresses the "fury," the wrath of God the Almighty, as a time of trouble and destruction. Romans 1:18 states, "for the wrath of God is revealed from heaven against all ungodliness and unrighteousness of men, who hold the truth in unrighteousness; because that which may be known of God is manifest in them." Without a moral compass, there are no absolutes, absolute truths that guide and determine what is right or what is wrong. There is no absolute in gender and marriage gets redefined. (We have seen these very acts happening today). Certainly, we should love others as Jesus loves them, but that does not mean we accept anything that blatantly contradicts the Bible.

The Cost of Losing Our Moral Compass.

Without a spiritual revival, our nation is doomed to excess moral decay. How much do we have to endure before we are humbled enough to fall on our knees and cry out to God for mercy? What would it take for this nation to humble itself, pray, and seek God's face? According to the CDC statistics (Center for Disease Control) in April 2021 does it take 30, 492, 334 Americans infected with COVID-19? Does it take over 553, 681 dying from COVID -19? Or does it take 5, 633 people to die in the last 7 days from COVID-19? How much more can we as a nation endure before we humble ourselves under the mighty hand of our Creator? Please wake up, America, for judgment is upon us.

Prayer for An Awakening in America.

Thank You, Father, for Your truth and Your great power. We praise Your great truth. Would You extend Your grace unto Your people, granting Your freedom, providing Your protection, and empowering with Your strength? We ask that You bring about an awakening in America as never seen before. We ask that Your name be proclaimed. We pray that many will come to know You as You have set us free from the clutching grasp of sin and death.

Old Testament Israel Lost its Moral Compass.

Israel also spiraled into moral decay, losing its moral compass. There are many examples in which Israel disobeyed God and went their own way, but God protected them and gave them chances to repent and turn to Him. Deuteronomy 1:7-8, "Turn you, and take your journey, and go into the mount of the Amorites, and unto all the places nigh thereunto, in the plain, in the hills, and in the vale, and in the south, and by the seaside, to the land of the Canaanites, and unto Lebanon, unto the great river, the river Euphrates. Behold I have set the land before you: go in and possess the land which the Lord sware unto your fathers, Abraham, Isaac, and Jacob, to give unto them and to their seed after them."

Let's Look at What America Has Lost.

We have lost our sense of right and wrong. Decisions are based on what works for me, on the convenience and compromise of our moral ethics and values. Ultimate standards are replaced by our own ethics. We bend the rules to satisfy our own selfish needs. We become a law unto ourselves. We reason that it is okay as long as no one finds out. We have lost our personal integrity; that is when a person's main characteristic is quality to the core. Without integrity being lived out, people are lying and breaking contracts; they will say whatever it takes to get a sale; people are cutthroat. A person's word means almost nothing now. (How far we have come from grace.) We have lost our ability to empathize; our self-centered orientation trumps the perspective of others. We have grown quite callous. We have quit asking how our choices are going to affect others. We no longer do unto others as we would have them do unto us. Matthew 7:12 states, "Therefore all things whatsoever ye would that men should do to you, do ye even so to them: for this is the law and the prophets." We have lost our conviction of commitment by breaking contracts in business (common practice). Giving up on marriage is the new norm. We take the easy path, not the right path. Lastly, we have lost our absolute standard of truth; people aren't reading and studying the scriptures like they used to. Previous generations wore out their Bibles, memorized verses more, and generally cared about what God's Word says. We have not followed in their footsteps and have become complacent in our walk of faith.

Five ways we can turn things around to strengthen the moral compass for our kids, the next generation:

1. *Understand the Sway of Your Conviction.* Kids sense your intensity about things; they can tell what matters to you. They feel it in your tone. Resolve to do what is right even if it costs you. You need to hunger in a way that pleases and honors God in front of your children. Be convinced and then live consistently to your moral compass.

2. *Grasp the Impact of Your Example.* Kids must hear and see consistently from their parents how to live morally. Children need to see that parents are called to a higher standard. Living the truth is your platform for teaching the truth.

3. *Hold Fast to the Anchor of God's Truth.* God has a plan we need to trust. When we are careless with His standards, we aren't simply breaking God's laws- they are breaking us. God wants us to read our Bibles daily. Teach children wrong from right and that it's not determined by consensus or convenience rather than conviction. God wants us to know and teach what the Bible says.

4. *Maximize the Strength of Your Reinforcement.* Remind children often about what is right and what is wrong. Coach them daily that God's way is the best way and that to compromise is wrong. Teach your children to do it in God's way. Reiterate the difference Jesus can make in a person's life. Repeat this message daily.

5. *Practice the Power of Prayer.* Pray that you as parents will keep a soft heart toward God and His Word. Pray that you will walk by faith and will conduct and live by what you believe. Ask God to convict you of callousness and compromise to His truth. Ask God to help you teach it to your children faithfully and caringly. Pray that your children will grow in their love for Jesus. Pray that His moral compass would stir in them.

God, We Need You.

As a nation, God, we need Your mercy and Your grace. Help us to desire righteousness more than rights, and to mirror sacrifice more than selfishness. You know our hearts; You know all our flaws and You understand us. Turn those weaknesses into strengths; bathe us in Your grace and mercy. Fill us with boldness to choose the kind of freedom that honors You and that will benefit all, rather than a few. Open our eyes to see others as You do, with godly potential and value. You have exercised nothing but fairness and faithfulness in Your treatment of America; even though we have turned our backs on You and have forgotten Your goodness. Draw us closer to You, bless us, and make us a great nation rich with Your biblical principles, a nation who reverences You. You are a good, good Father.

Let me tell you about my Jesus, the only hope for America, our eternal hope of glory. Help us to renew our minds, restore our hearts unto You, and rebuild our homes and communities, giving glory unto You.

Matthew 24: 8 says, "All these are the beginning of sorrows."

Chapter 15

God's Spirit Removed

The Bible clearly states that God will remove His spirit from the earth. This is the beginning of birth pains. As a woman goes into labor and experiences birth pains and then soon delivers her child, so shall this happen as God's appointed time draws near. Ephesians 4:30 states, "And grieve not the holy Spirit of God, whereby ye are sealed unto the day of redemption."

The Holy Spirit will be taken out of the world when He has done all that He can to save us, and we resist it or accept it. If we accept salvation, we will be sealed with the seal of the living God. If we deny it, we will be locked out of the ark like the people of Noah's day were. "And the Lord said, 'My spirit shall not always strive with man, for that he also is flesh: yet his days shall be a hundred and twenty years.'" Genesis 6:3.

Everything in the world is in distress. The signs of the times are threatening. Coming events cast their shadows. The Spirit of God is withdrawing from the earth, and calamity follows calamity by land and by sea. There are tempests, earthquakes, fires, floods, and murders of every caliber.

The "once-in-a-lifetime" and "never-before-seen" disasters are piling up on top of each other – one after another. The loudest voices being heard today say that nothing significant is happening. They tell you not to worry about the non-stop, horrific events taking place today. The proud, boastful, pleasure-seekers say, "All things continue as they were from the beginning." 2 Peter 3:4 states, "Knowing this first, that there shall come in the last days scoffers, walking after their own lusts, and saying, where is the promise of His coming? For since the fathers fell asleep, all things continue as they were from the beginning of the creation." Godless men who are void of knowledge say, "Tomorrow shall be as this day, and much more abundant." By these words, the scorners and rejecters of truth are putting people fast asleep into a false sense of carnal security. But we as children of God cry out unto our Father and declare His holiness. Isaiah 12:4 states, "And in that day shall ye say, Praise the Lord, call upon His name, declare His doings among the people, make mention that His name is exalted."

Many refuse to see that the signs of the end times that Jesus spoke of are happening before our very eyes. There are those who laugh at any notion that prophecy is being fulfilled in relation to the recent (1) 2018 historic fire season, the (2) 2018 historic hurricane season, the (3) 2017 and 2018 historic flooding, the (4) historic liberal and moral collapse of the churches, the (5) historic political divide and polarization in America, the (6) 2015 Obergefell v. Hodges and 2017

Pavan v. Smith US Supreme Court decisions that codified immorality and normalized sin in our nation, the (7) historic mass shootings in CA, PA, FL and other places and (8) the increasing tensions and problems facing the other nations around the world. How can anyone imagine that nothing significant is happening?

> The question of the Holy Spirit not being present during the tribulation results from a misunderstanding of 2 Thessalonians 2:7, which reads, "For the mystery of iniquity doth already work; only he who now letteth will let, until he be taken out of the way." Right now, prior to the tribulation, one of the ministries of the Holy Spirit is the restraint of evil. In verses 8 and 9, we learn that the restraining power of the Holy Spirit holds back the "lawless one" (Antichrist) so he is not revealed before God wills it. The passage says the Holy Spirit will no longer restrain the growth of evil, but that does not mean He will have no ministry whatsoever. In Acts 1:4–5 states, "And, being assembled together with them, commanded them that they should not depart from Jerusalem, but wait for the promise of the Father, which saith he, ye have heard of me. For John truly baptized with the Holy Ghost not many days hence."

Jesus promises that His disciples would soon be "baptized with water; but ye shall be baptized with the Holy Ghost not many days hence." Acts chapter 2:1 states, "And when the day of Pentecost was fully come, they were all with one accord in one place." We read about the miraculous event where people from all nations heard the disciples speaking and joyfully praising God in their own language. Acts 2: 7-13 states, "And they were all amazed and marveled, saying one to another Behold, are not all these which speak Galileans? And how we hear every man in their own tongue, wherein we were born? [Then how is it that each of us hears them in his own native language?] Parthians, Medes, and Elamites; and the dwellers in Mesopotamia, and in Judaea and Cappadocia, in Pontus, and Asia, Phrygia and Pamphylia in Egypt, and the parts of Libya about Cyrene; and strangers of Rome, Jews and proselytes. Cretans and Arabians, we do hear them speak in our tongues the wonderful works of God. And they were all amazed and were in doubt, saying one to another, What meaneth this? [they asked one another, "What does this mean?"] Others mocking said, these men are full of new wine."

That the disciples were not drunk but were in the right minds is quickly stated by Peter, who, speaking clearly and logically, explains what was happening:

Act 2:14-21, "But Peter stood up with the eleven, lifted up his voice and said to them, Ye men of Judaea, and all ye that dwell at Jerusalem, be this known unto you, and hearken to my words: For these are not drunken as you suppose, seeing that it is but the third hour of the day. But this that that which was spoken by the prophet Joel; And it shall come to pass in the last days, saith God, I will pour out my Spirit upon all flesh: and your sons and your daughters shall prophesy, and your young men shall see visions, and your old men shall dream dreams. And on my servants, and on my handmaidens I will pour out in those days of my Spirit; and they shall prophesy: And I will show wonders in the heaven above, and signs in the earth beneath; blood and fire and vapour of smoke. The sun shall be turned to darkness and the moon into blood before the coming of the great and notable day of the Lord come." And it shall come to pass, that whosoever shall call on the name of the Lord shall be saved."

Jesus' promise is fulfilled. In verses 38 and 39, it is written that Peter replied, "Then Peter said unto them, Repent and be baptized, every one of you, in the name of Jesus Christ for the remission of sins, and you shall receive the gift of the Holy Ghost. For the promise is unto you, and to your children, and to all that are far off, even as many as the Lord our God shall call."

The indwelling of the Holy Spirit is thus assured for every born-again believer, and nowhere in Scripture is that promise rescinded. Regeneration is the Spirit's work; without Him, no one is saved. If the Spirit were not present during the tribulation, no one could be saved. But the fact is that a multitude that no one can number is saved during the tribulation (Revelation 7:9–14). "After this I beheld, and lo, a great multitude which no man could number, of all nations and all kindreds, and people and tongues, stood before the throne, and before the Lamb, clothed with white robes, and palms in their hands. And cried with a loud voice, saying, Salvation to our God which sitteth upon the throne, and unto the Lamb. And all the angels stood round about the throne, and about the elders and the four beasts, and fell before the throne on their faces, and worshipped God. Saying, Amen: Blessing, and glory and wisdom, and thanksgiving, and honor, and power and might, be unto our God forever and ever. Amen. And one of the elders answered, saying unto me, what are these which are arrayed in white robes? And whence came they? And I said unto him, Sir, thou knowest. And He said to me, these are they which came out of the great tribulation, and have washed their robes, and made them white in the blood of the Lamb."

Therefore, those who come to Jesus during the tribulation period will also be indwelt by the Holy Spirit. Give glory to God for making that provision, because tribulation saints will need the guidance and direction of the Spirit during that troubled time.

Another good reason that the Spirit must be present during the tribulation is that He is omnipresent (ever present). Since He is always everywhere, He must be in the world during the tribulation.

At some point, only God knows when the restraining influence of the Holy Spirit will be removed, the Antichrist will be revealed to an unwitting and unsuspecting world, and the tribulation period will begin.

Christ will remove all born-again believers from the earth in an event known as the rapture (1 Thessalonians 4:13-18; 1 Corinthians 15:51-54). At the judgment seat of Christ, these believers will be rewarded for good works and faithful service during their time on earth or will lose rewards, but not eternal life, for lack of service and obedience (1 Corinthians 3:11-15; 2 Corinthians 5:10). God's Word states in 2 Corinthians 5:10, "For we must all appear before the judgment seat of

Christ; that every one may receive the things done in his body, according to that he hath done, whether it be good or bad."

The Antichrist (the beast) will come into power and will sign a covenant with Israel for seven years (Daniel 9:27). "And he shall confirm the covenant with many for one week: and in the midst of the week, he shall cause the sacrifice and the oblation to cease, and for the overspreading of abominations he shall make it desolate, even unto the consummation, and that determined shall be poured upon the desolate." This seven-year period is known as the "tribulation." During the tribulation, there will be terrible wars, famines, plagues, and natural disasters. God will be pouring out His wrath against sin, evil, and wickedness. The tribulation will include the appearance of the four horsemen of the Apocalypse, and the seven seal, trumpet, and bowl judgments.

About halfway through the seven years, the Antichrist will break the peace covenant with Israel and make war against it. Matthew 24:15 states, "When ye therefore shall see the abomination of desolation, spoken of by Daniel the prophet, stand in the holy place, (whoso readeth, let him understand)." The Antichrist will commit "the abomination of desolation" (this is one of the signs of the end, when the antichrist sets up an abomination in the holy place and will command people to worship it. This object of disgust, an idol, will cause desolation, causing those in Judea to flee to the mountains), mentioned in

Matthew 24:16 and set up an image of himself to be worshiped in the Jerusalem temple (Daniel 9:27; 2 Thessalonians 2:3-10), which will have been rebuilt. The second half of the tribulation is known as "the great tribulation" (Revelation 7:14) and "the time of Jacob's trouble" (Jeremiah 30:7).

At the end of the seven-year tribulation, the Antichrist will launch a final attack on Jerusalem, culminating in the battle of Armageddon. Jesus Christ will return, destroy the Antichrist and his armies, and cast them into the lake of fire (Revelation 19:11-21). Christ will then bind Satan in the Abyss for 1,000 years and He will rule His earthly kingdom for this thousand-year period (Revelation 20:16). "And I saw an angel come down from heaven, having the key to the bottomless pit and a great chain in his hand. And he laid hold on the dragon, that old serpent, which is the devil, and Satan, and bound him a thousand years, and cast him into the bottomless pit and shut him up, and set a seal upon him, that he should deceive the nations no more, till the thousand years should be fulfilled: and after that, he must be loosed a little season. And I saw thrones, and they sat upon them, and judgment was given unto them: and I saw the souls of them that were beheaded for the witness of Jesus, and for the word of God, and which had not worshipped the beast, neither his image, neither had received his mark upon their foreheads or in their hands; and they lived and reigned with Christ a thousand years. But the rest of the dead lived not again until the thousand years were finished.

This is the first resurrection. Blessed and holy is he that hath part in the first resurrection: on such the second death hath no power, but they shall be priests of God and of Christ and shall reign with Him a thousand years."

At the end of the thousand years, Satan will be released, defeated again, and then cast into the lake of fire (Revelation 20:7-10) for eternity. "And when the thousand years are expired, Satan shall be loosed out of his prison, and shall go out to deceive the nations which are in the four quarters of the earth, Gog, and Magog, to gather them together to battle: the number of whom is as the sand of the sea. And they went up from the breadth of the earth and compassed the camp of the saints about, and the beloved city: and fire came down from God out of heaven and devoured them. And the devil that deceived them was cast into the lake of fire and brimstone, where the beast and the false prophet are, and shall be tormented day and night forever and ever."

Christ then judges all unbelievers (Revelation 20:1115) at the great white throne judgment, casting them all into the lake of fire. "And I saw a great white throne, and Him that sat on it, from whose face the earth and the heaven fled away; and there was found no place for them. And I saw the dead, small and great, stand before God: and the books were opened: and another book was opened, which is the book of life: and the dead were judged out of those things which were written in the books, according to their works. And the sea gave up the dead which were in it, and death and hell delivered up the dead which were in them: and they were judged every man according to their works. And death and hell were cast into the lake of fire. This is the second death. And whosoever was not found written in the book of life was cast into the lake of fire." Christians will not be present; they will participate in a separate judgement known as the Judgment Seat of Christ, because the righteousness of Christ is credited to every believer.

Christ will then usher in a new heaven and new earth and the New Jerusalem, the eternal dwelling place of believers. There will be no more sin, sorrow, or death. (Revelation 21:1-2) states, "Now I saw a new heaven and a new earth, for the first heaven and the first earth had passed away. Also, there was no more sea. Then I, John, saw the holy city, New Jerusalem, coming down out of heaven from God, prepared as a bride adorned for her husband."

> (Revelation 21:10), "And He carried me away in the Spirit to a great and high mountain, and showed me the great city, the holy Jerusalem, descending out of heaven from God."

> (Revelation 21:22), "But I saw no temple in it, for the Lord God Almighty and the Lamb are its temple."

The only proof I need of the Rapture of the Church is the fact that God is going to remove the Holy Spirit from the earth in the last days, and we are sealed with the Holy Spirit.

> Referring to 2 Thessalonians 2:7, it states, "For the mystery of iniquity doth already work: only he who now letteth will let, until he be taken out of the way." This passage is thought to foretell the removal of the Holy Spirit from the world, and since the Holy Spirit is sealed within us, logic says we must go. It is a hint of the Rapture of the Church before the Antichrist is fully revealed. The Holy Spirit does have a ministry during the End Times. He is just not sealed within believers like He is with us. It is more like Old Testament times.

There are also other valid reasons why the Church must disappear before the Great Tribulation. The fact is that the pre-tribulation rapture is the only position that can be supported by a strict, literal interpretation of Scripture. But recognize that the debate over the existence or timing of the rapture is not based on logic, but emotion.

The real issue is the nature and extent of God's Grace. It does not take a genius to know that we deserve to be punished for our sins. Somehow the idea that Jesus took all our punishment for us does not seem fair, especially to those of us who were taught that we must bear the consequences of our behavior. Grace is counterintuitive to the mind trained to believe in justice and fairness, because it lets us escape, to "get away with it." It is not fair. We should get what we deserve. But His marvelous grace and mercy has bought our salvation.

Those who deny the pre-tribulation rapture often point to the early church. They were saved by grace too, but they still suffered horrible persecution. Why should we escape? These folks need to really study the Seven Letters of Revelation, chapters 2 through 3, which state as a prophetic chronology of church history. The Church of the persecution is personified in the Letter to Smyrna. It was not promised any relief, only admonished to hold on through the reign of ten Caesars (250 years) even until death to receive life. In fact, none of the first three letters promised relief. It was not till the Letter of Thyatira that any hope of escape was offered, and only the Letter to Philadelphia promises to keep us from the time of trial altogether.

There are no modern equivalents to Ephesus, Smyrna, or Pergamos. I believe they served a specific purpose designed to accelerate the early growth of the Church and occupy a special place in God's heart. They might be the ones depicted in Revelation 6:9-11.

But Thyatira symbolizes the Catholic Church, Sardis the mainline Protestants, Philadelphia the Evangelical Church, and Laodicea the Apostates. All four of them are still on Earth today, and in three of the four, escape is promised to at least some. Only Laodicea is omitted.

The reality is that the Grace of God is beyond the ability of our guilt-laden minds to comprehend, and for many, it is too much to even hope for. When our dreams exceed the limits of our imaginations, we are more likely to fear the consequences of failure than to anticipate the rewards of success. A post-tribulation rapture, or even none, becomes the safer alternative.

> 1 Thessalonians 5: 2-3 states, "For yourselves know perfectly that the day of the Lord so cometh as a thief in the night. For when they shall say peace and safety; then sudden destruction cometh upon them, as travail upon a woman with child; and they shall not escape."

"The Holy Spirit illuminates the minds of people, makes us yearn for God, and takes spiritual truth and makes it understandable to us." – Billy Graham

Chapter 16

America Judged (God's Wrath Revealed)

When we discuss the weight of sin in our lives, thoughts and actions that are not in alignment with God's perfect will for us, we must know that there is a Judgement Day coming in which we will give an account for what we have done as His children. Will you hear Him say, "Well done, thou good and faithful servant?" That is our eternal hope of glory, to run the race with patience and finish the race of faith, to reach forward to the prize before us: eternal life with our Savior.

Here are five biblical truths about the wrath of God:

1. *God's wrath is just.*

   It has become common for many to argue that the God of the Old Testament is a God of judgement and that His wrath is justified to rid the stain of sin that has overshadowed our lives. He gave us our own will to choose the way, the truth, and the life through the blood of Jesus, who shed His precious blood for the remission of our sins. However, biblical authors have no such problem.

In fact, God's wrath is said to be in perfect accord with God's justice. Paul writes in Romans 2:5, "But after thy hardness and impenitent heart treasurest up unto thyself wrath against the day of wrath and revelation of the righteous judgement of God." God's wrath is His love in action against sin. Similarly, Proverbs 24:12-13 says, "And because iniquity shall abound, the love of many shall wax cold. But he that shall endure unto the end, the same shall be saved, and this gospel of the kingdom shall be preached in all the world for a witness unto all nations; and then shall the end come. Does not he who keeps watch over your soul know it, and will he not repay man according to his work?"

2. *God's wrath is to be feared.*

God's wrath is to be feared because all have sinned and fallen short of the glory of God. Romans 3:23 states, "For all have sinned and come short of the glory of God."

Romans 5:1 says, "Therefore being justified by faith, we have peace with God through our Lord Jesus Christ." Jeremiah 32:17 reads, "Ah Lord God! behold, thou hast made the heaven and the earth by thy great power and stretched out arm, and there is nothing too hard for thee." Matthew 25:46. States, "And these shall go away into everlasting punishment: but the righteous into life eternal."

3. *God's wrath is consistent in the Old and New Testaments.*

It is common to think of the Old Testament God as mean, harsh, and wrath-filled, and the God of the New Testament as kind, patient, and loving. Neither of these portraits are representative of Scripture's teaching on the wrath of God.

We find immensely fearful descriptions of the wrath of God in both the Old and the New Testament. Here are just a few examples:

Jeremiah 10:24 says, "O Lord, correct me, but with judgment; not in thine anger, lest thou bring me to nothing." In Romans 1:18 we read, "For the wrath of God is revealed from heaven against all ungodliness and unrighteousness of men, who hold the truth in unrighteousness." Thessalonians 2: 8 states, "And then shall that Wicked be revealed, whom the Lord shall consume with the spirit of his mouth and shall destroy with the brightness of his coming." God must act justly and judge sin, otherwise God would not be God.

Behold the vengeance of the Lord! Wrath has gone forth, a whirling tempest; it will burst upon the head of the wicked." Jeremiah 30:23 says, "Behold the whirlwind of the Lord goeth forth with fury, a continuing whirlwind: it shall fall with pain upon the head of the wicked." Nahum 1:2 reads, "God is jealous, and the Lord revengeth; the Lord revengeth, and is furious; the Lord will take vengeance on his adversaries and he reserveth wrath for his enemies."

Romans 1:18 states, "For the wrath of God is revealed from heaven against all ungodliness and unrighteousness of men, who hold the truth in unrighteousness."

Romans 19:15 reads, "We then that are strong ought to bear the infirmities of the weak, and not to please ourselves."

4. *God's wrath is His love in action against sin.*

This is counterintuitive, but hear me out. God is love, and God does all things for His glory. 1 John 4:8 states, "He that loveth not knoweth not God; for God is love." Romans 11:36 reads, "For of him, and through him, and to him, are all things: to whom be glory forever. Amen." He loves His glory above all (and that is a good thing!). Therefore, God rules the world in such a way that brings maximum glory to Himself. This means that God must act justly and judge sin (i.e., respond with wrath), otherwise God would not be God. God's love for His glory motivates His wrath against sin. Admittedly, God's love for His own glory is a most sobering reality for many and not good news for sinners. It is, after all, "a fearful thing to fall into the hands of the living God" (Hebrews 10:31).

5. *God's wrath is satisfied in Christ.*

Because of Christ, God can rightly call sinners justified. Romans 3:26, "To declare, I say, at this time his righteousness: that he might be just, and the justifier of him which believeth in Jesus." Here we have the ultimate good news: "Christ Jesus came into the world to save sinners." 1 Timothy 1:15 states, "This is a faithful saying, and worthy of all acceptation, that Christ Jesus came into the world to save sinners: of whom I am chief." Because of Christ, God can rightly call sinners justified. Romans 3:26 says, "To declare, I say, at this time his righteousness: that he might be just, and the justifier of him which believeth in Jesus." God has done what we could not do, and He has done what we did not deserve.

Charles Wesley rightly exulted in this good news:

And can it be that I should gain
An interest in the Savior's blood?
Died he for me, who caused his pain!
For me, who him to death pursued?

Amazing love! How can it be
That thou, my God, shouldest die for me?

Wrath is defined as "the emotional response to perceived wrong and injustice," often translated as "anger," "indignation," "vexation," or "irritation." Both humans and God express wrath. But there is vast difference between the wrath of God and the wrath of man. God's wrath is holy and always justified; man's is never holy and rarely justified. In the Old Testament, the wrath of God is a divine response to human sin and disobedience. Idolatry was most often the occasion for divine wrath. Psalm 78:56-66 describes Israel's idolatry. Psalm 78:56 states, "Yet they tempted and provoked the most high God and kept not his testimonies." Psalm 78:58 says, "For they provoked Him to anger with their high places and moved him to jealousy with their graven images." The wrath of God is consistently directed towards those who do not follow His will (Deuteronomy 1:26-46; Joshua 7:1; Psalm 2:1-6). The Old Testament prophets often wrote of a day in the future, the "day of wrath." Zephaniah 1:14-15 states, "The great day of the Lord is near, it is near, and hasteth greatly, even the voice of the day of the Lord: the mighty man shall cry there bitterly. That day is a day of wrath, a day of trouble and distress, a day of wasteness and desolation, a day of darkness and gloominess, a day of clouds and thick darkness." God's wrath against sin and disobedience is perfectly justified because His plan for humanity is holy and perfect, just as God Himself is holy and perfect.

God provided a way to gain divine favor and repentance, which turns God's wrath away from the sinner. To reject that perfect plan is to reject God's love, mercy, grace, and favor and incur His righteous wrath.

The New Testament also supports the concept of God as a God of wrath who judges sin. The story of the rich man and Lazarus speaks of the judgment of God and serious consequences for the unrepentant sinner (Luke 16:19– 31). There was a rich man and a beggar named Lazarus; Lazarus desired to be fed with the crumbs from the rich man's table. He died and was carried by the angels into Abraham's bosom; the rich man also died and was buried and in hell lifted his eyes, being in torment, and begged for a drop of water to cool his tongue in his torment. For he had the finer things in life, and now that he had died and was buried, he would spend eternity in hell. (He gained the whole world, only to lose his own soul.) John 3:36 says, "He that believes on the Son hath everlasting life, and he that believeth not the Son shall not see life; but the wrath of God abideth on him." The one who believes in the Son will not suffer God's wrath for his sin, because the Son took God's wrath upon Himself when He died in our place on the cross.

See Romans 5:6–11. Those who do not believe in the Son, who do not receive Him as Savior, will be judged on the day of wrath. Romans 2:5–6 reads, "But after thy hardness and impenitent heart treasurest up unto thyself wrath against the day of wrath and revelation of the righteous judgment of God. Who will render to every man according to his deeds."

Conversely, human wrath is warned against in Romans 12:19, Ephesians 4:26, and Colossians 3:8-10. God alone can avenge, because His vengeance is perfect and holy, whereas man's wrath is sinful, opening him up to demonic influence. For the Christian, anger and wrath are inconsistent with our new nature, which is the nature of Christ Himself. 2 Corinthians 5:17 states, "Therefore if any man be in Christ, he is a new creature: old things are passed away; behold all things are become new."

To realize freedom from the domination of wrath, the believer needs the Holy Spirit to sanctify and cleanse his heart of feelings of wrath and anger. Romans 8:5-8 shows victory over sin in the life of one who is living in the Spirit. Philippians 4:4-7 tells us that the mind controlled by the Spirit is filled with peace. "Rejoice in the Lord always; and again, I say, Rejoice. Let your moderation be known unto all men, the Lord is at hand. Be careful for nothing; but in everything by prayer and supplication with thanksgiving let your requests be known unto God. And the peace of God, which passeth all understanding, shall keep your hearts and minds through Christ Jesus."

The wrath of God is a fearsome and terrifying thing. Only those who have been covered by the blood of Christ, shed for us on the cross, can be assured that God's wrath will never fall on them. Thessalonians 5:9, "For God hath not appointed us to wrath, but to obtain salvation by our Lord Jesus Christ, who died for us, that whether we wake or sleep, we should live." Romans 1:18 states, "For the wrath of God is revealed from heaven against all ungodliness and unrighteousness of men, who hold the truth in unrighteousness."

Revelation 6:8 says, "And I looked and behold a pale horse: and his name that sat on him was death, and Hell followed with him. And power was given unto them over the fourth part of the earth, to kill with sword, and with hunger, and with death, and with the beasts of the earth."

Chapter Seventeen

Alpha and Omega, "The Beginning and End"

Jesus calls Himself the Alpha and Omega three times in the book of Revelation (Revelation 1:8; 21:6; 22:13). In the Greek language, the original language of the New Testament, alpha was the first letter of the alphabet and omega was the last letter. Jesus further elaborates the meaning.

In Revelation 22:13, He refers to Himself as, "The Alpha and Omega, the first and the last, the beginning and the end." This is also mentioned in Revelation 21:6.

Theologically, as the Alpha and the Omega, Jesus refers to Himself as eternal. From beginning to end, Jesus has always existed and will always exist. This is an attribute unique to God, meaning that Jesus equates Himself with the eternal God the Father.

Jesus did this in His earthly ministry as well, being taught and teaching in the temple as a 12-year-old boy Luke 2: 41-52 reads, "Now his parents went to Jerusalem every year at the feast of the Passover. And when he was twelve years old, they went up to Jerusalem after the custom of the feast. And when they had fulfilled the days, as they returned, the child Jesus tarried behind in Jerusalem; and Joseph and his mother knew not of it. But they, supposing him to have been in the company, went on a day's journey; and they sought him among their kinsfolk and acquaintances. And when they found him not, they turned back again to Jerusalem, seeking him. And it came to pass that after three days they found him in the temple, sitting in the midst of the doctors, both hearing them, and asking them questions. And all that heard him were astonished at his understanding and answers. And when they saw him, they were amazed: and his mother said unto him, Son, why hast thou thus dealt with us? Behold, thy father and I have sought thee sorrowing. And he said unto them, How is it that ye sought me? Wist ye not that I must be about my Father's business? And they understood not the saying which he spoke unto them. And he went down with them, and came to Nazareth, and was subject unto them: but his mother kept all these sayings in her heart. And Jesus increased in wisdom and stature, and in favor with God and man."

And Jesus telling the religious leaders, said unto them, "Verily, verily I say unto you before Abraham was, I am." John 8:58.

In Exodus 3:14 they understood His statement as a claim to be the Lord, "I am." "And God said unto Moses, I AM THAT I AM: and he said, thus shalt thou say unto the children of Israel, I AM hath sent me unto you."

Further, as Alpha and Omega, Jesus connects Himself with statements of God from the Old Testament in Isaiah 44:6 says, "Thus saith the LORD the King of Israel, and his redeemer the LORD of hosts; I am the first, and I am the last; and beside me there is no God." Isaiah 48:12 includes, "Hearken unto me, O Jacob and Israel, my called; I am he; I am the first, I also am the last." The Old Testament also highlights the use of first and last as marking the beginning and the end of something, as an example, 1 Chronicles 29:29 states, "Now the acts of David the king, first and last, behold, they are written in the book of Samuel the seer, and in the book of Nathan the prophet, and in the book of Gad, the seer." In the context, it clearly indicates, "from first to last" refers to "from beginning to end," a feature used seven times in 1 and 2 Chronicles. Conceivably, the first time this phrase is used summarizes it best.

Revelation 1:8 reads, "I am Alpha and Omega, the beginning and the ending, saith the Lord, which is, and which was, and which is to come, the Almighty."

Jesus is the eternal One and the Almighty will one day return to fulfill the remaining prophecies of scripture. Jesus is the Alpha and the Omega in His eternal nature, His role in creation, His sustaining of the world/universe, and in His fulfillment as the Messiah. Those who read His Word as He refers to Himself as the Alpha and the Omega in Revelation find One who is King of Kings and Lord of Lords, Who will one day make all things new (Revelation 21-22). Revelation 22:13 says, "I am Alpha and Omega, the beginning and the end, the first and the last." Revelation 19:16 reads, "And he hath on his vesture and on his thigh a name written, KING OF KINGS, AND LORD OF LORDS." Revelation 21:1 states, "And I saw a new heaven and a new earth: for the first heaven and the first earth were passed away; and there was no more sea." Revelation 21:5, "And he that sat upon the throne said, Behold, I make all things new..."

The Greek letters Alpha and Omega (A and ω), spoken four times by Jesus to the apostle John (Revelation 1:8, 11, 21:6, 22:13), reveal several Bible truths concerning Himself. These truths revolve around His character, the power and authority He possesses, and His role in carrying out God the Father's awesome goals.

"In the beginning was the word, and the word was with God, and the word was God." John 1:1

Revelation 1:11 is a slight variation of verse 8, as the Lord states He is "the first and the last." Interestingly, the final occurrence of these two Greek letters combines the previous three times they are recorded.

"I am Alpha and Omega, the Beginning, and the End, the First and the Last" (Revelation 22:13).

All this begs the following question. How is Jesus Christ the first (beginning) and last (ending) of what God is doing?

The First (Alpha)

The Apostle John reveals that God the Father, through God the Son (Jesus), created all things. The Lord not only brought into existence the physical universe but also the first humans. He additionally created the invisible spirit world (John 1:1-3, Ephesians 3:9, etc.) with its many angels.

The Apostle Paul declares that Jesus was the first person to announce "so great a salvation" to humanity (Hebrews 2:3). His words were later confirmed and amplified by the apostles.

Jesus is the first or head (beginning) of the spiritual organism known as the Church of God. This group is a collection of all those who ever lived who were converted and will be in the first resurrection (Ephesians 1:22, 4:15, 23, Colossians 1:18).

Christ lived a physical life and died but was resurrected from the dead. He is the first (the Alpha, first fruits or firstborn) of countless others who will also be resurrected and changed into an eternal spirit being (1 Corinthians 15:20 23, Colossians 1:15 18, Revelation 1:5).

The Last (Omega)

Since Jesus is God and was with God in the beginning (John 1:1-2), He has always existed and there was never a time when Jesus did not exist, because God is eternal and has no beginning nor does He have an ending. Jesus' body died, but His spirit could not. At His death on the cross He cried out to God, "Father, into your hands I commend my spirit!" And having said this he breathed his last (Luke 23:46). It was just after Jesus had received the sour wine, He said, "It is finished," and He bowed His head and gave up His spirit (John 19:30). So the spirit cannot die, even though Jesus' earthly body did. His spirit went back to the Father Who received it, and today, He is at the right hand of the Father and is in all His glory. He was in the beginning and part of the beginning of creation, but He will also be at the end of this age when it will be said that the world has now become "the Kingdoms of our Lord and of his Christ, and he will reign forever and ever" (Revelation 11:15). For those who have trusted in Christ, death is not the end, it is just the beginning, and it is the time when we will be in the very presence of God (Revelation 21:3; 22:4).

Adam, the first human created, sinned. His sin caused humanity to be cut off from their Creator, resulting in death passing on to all humans (1 Corinthians 15:21 22). Jesus, as the second or last Adam, lived a perfect life in obedience to the Father. His sacrifice makes possible a resurrection into eternal life for all those who repent and live a life of overcoming (verses 20 24).

The Lord, after the order of Melchisedek (Hebrews 5:5 6), is the final (Omega) and greatest High Priest. As man's spiritual advocate before the Father, He lives to intercede on our behalf and to make possible the perfecting of our character for eternity (10:14, 21-22).

Jesus, as a member of the Godhead, was tasked with beginning and finishing the Father's great plan for mankind. When He has fully ended His work, and "cleaned up" all that exists so that what remains is sinless and perfect, "He shall have delivered up the kingdom to Him Who is God and Father . . ." (1 Corinthians 15:24, see also Revelation 21:27).

Profound Meanings

The first two sentences Jesus speaks to the Apostle John (Revelation 1:8, 11), as well as two others (21:6, 22:13), use the Greek letters Alpha and Omega to convey multiple spiritual truths.

Alpha and Omega, along with the declaration he is "the Almighty" (Revelation 1:8), clearly shows Jesus is divine and a member of the Godhead. The Greek word translated as Almighty, Strong's Concordance #G3841, refers to God as a universal sovereign who is all-powerful and ruler of all. These letters testify, from eternity to eternity, to His unchangeable righteous character.

These Greek alphabet letters additionally convey that the Lord is the first cause of all things in the universe. He created all things, whether visible or invisible. Lastly, Alpha and Omega assure us Christ, as the one who began the Father's plan to create countless holy beings, will perfectly carry it out to the end.

First Man Adam

In the first book of the Bible, Genesis, we read that when the first man, Adam, sinned, he died positionally; he was totally dead to God: spirit, soul, and body. Thereafter his position was manifested in his condition; he began to die experientially. In God's mercy, it was some 930 years before Adam fully experienced the inevitable outcome of the position of death. Adam, as head of the human race, took all of humanity into that position of death through disobedience in the garden. 1 Corinthians 15:22 reads, "For in Adam all die." All in Adam have their lives and therefore are "by nature the children of wrath" (Ephesians 2:3). Adamic life is the source of sin in everyone, whether unsaved or saved (Romans 5:12).

Due to the Fall, Adam became flesh, not only his body, but his soul and spirit as well. Genesis 6:3 reads, "My spirit shall not always strive with man, for that he also is flesh." Hence the race spawned by Adam and Eve is flesh. "That which is born of flesh is flesh" (John 3:6). It is not that the natural man has flesh or is in the condition of flesh; he is flesh. Paul wrote in Romans 7:18, "For I know that in me dwelleth no good thing." As a believer, Paul was indwelt by his Adamic life, the old man, and he assumed full responsibility for his sinful actions. When we are born again, we get a new nature, for we are a new creature in Christ Jesus. 2 Corinthians 5:17 reads, "Therefore if any man be in Christ, he is a new creature: old things are passed away; behold all things become new."

> Romans 10:9-10 says, "That if thou shalt confess with thy mouth the Lord, Jesus, and shalt believe in thine heart that God hath raised him from the dead, thou shalt be saved, For with the heart man believeth unto righteousness; and with the mouth confession is made unto salvation."

We are Born to Die.

We are born into the world as a sinner; we must trust Jesus through confessing our sins and believing in His death, burial, and resurrection to be born again. Scripture tells us in Ecclesiastes 3:1-8, "To everything there is a season, and a time to every purpose under the heaven: a time to be born, and a time to die; a time to plant, and a time to pluck up that which is planted; a time to kill, and a time to heal; a time to break down, and a time to build up; a time to weep, and a time to laugh; a time to mourn and a time to dance; a time to cast away stones, and a time to gather stones together; a time to embrace, and a time to refrain from embracing; a time to get, and a time to lose; a time to keep, and a time to cast away; a time to rend, and a time to sew; a time to keep silence, and a time to speak; a time to love, and a time to hate, a time of war, and a time of peace."

Hebrews 9:27 reads, "And as it is appointed unto men once to die, but after this the judgment:"

Chapter Eighteen

A Legacy of Truth

What is in a name? What is in a legacy? What is the meaning and origin of a legacy of truth? Let us start with what is in a name, the name of Jesus, the name above all others. Isaiah 9:6 states, "For unto us a child is born, unto us a son is given: and the government shall be upon his shoulder: and his name shall be called Wonderful, Counselor, The Mighty God, The Everlasting Father, The Prince of Peace." Jesus has many names and each one represents his character and majesty. The Trinity consists of Father, Son, and Holy Spirit (three in one).

> Psalms 148:13 reads, "Let them praise the name
> of the Lord: for his name alone is excellent: his
> glory is above the earth and heaven."

What's in a Name?

Jehovah- (the eternal One, the unchangeable One, who was, and is, and is to come) Jehovah Jireh- my provider (the Lord will provide) Genesis 22:12-14

Jehovah Nissi- (the Lord is our banner) Exodus 17:8-15

Jehovah Rapha- (the Lord who heals) Exodus 15:22-26

Jehovah Rohi- (the Lord is my shepherd) Psalms 23:1

Jehovah Shalom- (the Lord my peace) Judges 6:24

Jehovah Tsidkenu- (the Lord my righteousness) Jeremiah 23:6

Jehovah Shammah- (the Lord is there for me) Ezekiel 48:35

The Names of God in the Old Testament

El Shaddai (Lord God Almighty)

El Elyon (the Most High God)

Adonai (Lord Master)

Yahweh (Lord Jehovah)

El Olam (the Everlasting God)

Elohim (God)

Qanna (Jealous)

As we learn more about who Jesus is and what His name represents, we fall more in love with His character. Throughout scripture, God reveals Himself to us through His names. When we study His Word, we can better understand who God really is. The meanings behind God's names reveal His central personality and nature of the One Who bears them. To hallow a thing is to make it holy or to set it apart to be exalted as being worthy of absolute devotion. To hallow the name of God is to reverence Him with complete devotion and loving admiration. We should never take His name lightly but always rejoice in it and think deeply upon its true meaning.

We will examine others in the Bible whose names represented their character and how their faith was tested and tried, yet they believed God and were motivated to carry out His commands.

Hebrews Heroes of Faith (Hebrews 11)

(1) Now faith is the substance of things hoped for, the evidence of things not seen.

(2) For by it the elders obtained a good report.

(3) Through faith we understand that the worlds were framed by the word of God, so that things which are seen were not made of things which do appear.

(4)By faith Abel offered unto God a more excellent sacrifice than Cain, by which he obtained witness that he was righteous, God testifying of his gifts: and by it he being dead yet speaketh.

(5) By faith Enoch was translated that he should not see death; and was not found, because God had translated him: for before his translation he had this testimony, that he pleased God.

(6) But without faith it is impossible to please Him: for he, that cometh to God must believe that He is, and that He is a rewarder of them that diligently seek Him.

(7) By faith Noah, being warned of God of things not seen as yet, moved with fear, prepared an ark to the saving of his house; by which he condemned the world, and became heir of the righteousness which is by faith.

(8) By faith Abraham, when he was called to go out into a place which he should after receiving for an inheritance, obeyed; and he went out, not knowing whether he went.

(9) By faith he sojourned in the land of promise, as in a strange country, dwelling in tabernacles with Isaac and Jacob, the heirs with him of the same promise:

(10) For he looked for a city which hath foundations, whose builder and maker is God.

(11) Through faith also Sara herself received strength to conceive seed and was delivered of a child when she was past age because she judged him faithful who had promised.

(12) Therefore, sprang there even one, and him as good as dead, so many as the stars of the sky in multitude, and as the sand which is by the seashore innumerable.

(13) These all died in faith, not having received the promises, but having seen them afar off, and were persuaded of them, and embraced them, and confessed that they were strangers and pilgrims on the earth.

(14) For those that say such things declare plainly that they seek a country.

(15) And truly, if they had been mindful of that country from whence they came out, they might have had the opportunity to have returned.

(16) But now they desire a better country, that is, a heavenly: wherefore God is not ashamed to be called their God: for he hath prepared for them a city.

(17) By faith, Abraham, when he was tried, offered up Isaac: and he that had received the promises offered up his only begotten son.

(18) Of whom it was said, that in Isaac shall thy seed be called:

(19) Accounting that God was able to raise him up, even from the dead; from whence also he received him in a figure.

(20) By faith Isaac blessed Jacob and Esau concerning things to come.

(21) By faith Jacob, when he was dying, blessed both the sons of Joseph; and worshiped, leaning upon the top of his staff.

(22) By faith Joseph, when he died, made mention of the departing of the children of Israel; and gave commandment concerning his bones.

(23) By faith Moses, when he was born, was hidden for three months of his parents, because they saw he was a proper child; and they were not afraid of the king's commandment.

(24) By faith Moses, when he was young, refused to be called the son of Pharaoh's daughter.

(25) Choosing rather to suffer affliction with the people of God, than to enjoy the pleasures of sin for a season.

(26) Esteeming the reproach of Christ greater riches than the treasures in Egypt: for he had respect unto the recompence of the reward.

(27) By faith he forsook Egypt, not fearing the wrath of the king: for he endured, as seeing him who is invisible.

(28) Through faith he kept the Passover, and the sprinkling of blood, lest he that destroyed the firstborn should touch them.

(29) By faith they passed through the red sea as by dry land: which the Egyptians assaying to do were drowned.

(30) By faith, the walls of Jericho fell, after they were compassed for about seven days.

(31) By faith, the harlot Rahab perished not with them that believed not when she had received the spies with peace.

(32) And what shall I say? For the time would fail me to tell of Gideon, and of Barak, and of Samson, and of Jephthah, of David also, and Samuel, and of the prophets:

(33) Who through faith subdued kingdoms, wrought righteousness, obtained promises, stopped the mouth of lions,

(34) Quenched the violence of fire, escaped the edge of the sword, out of weakness were made strong, waxed valiant in fight, turned to fight the armies of aliens.

(35) Women received their dead raised to life again; and others were tortured, not accepting deliverance; that they might obtain a better resurrection:

(36) And others had trials of cruel mocking and scourings, yea moreover of bonds and imprisonment.

(37) They were stoned, they were sawn asunder, were tempted, were slain with the sword: they wandered about

in sheepskins and goatskins; being destitute, afflicted, tormented.

(38) Of whom the world was not worthy:) they wandered in deserts, and in mountains, and in dens and caves of the earth.

(39) And these all, having obtained a good report through faith, received not the promise:

(40) God having provided some better thing for us, that they without us should not be made perfect.

What's in a Legacy?

The certainty of death brings clarity to the living of life. For every single one of us, our days will soon be over, and the wise among us will take this reality to heart (Ecclesiastes 7:2). Our mortality ought to awaken us to the truth that as we walk this earthly sod, we are all leaving a legacy.

Our lives are canvases on which we are painting—and those pictures will remain after we have gone. The question is not whether we will leave a legacy but what kind we will leave. Solomon presents the options starkly: "The memory of the just is blessed, but the name of the wicked shall rot" (Proverbs 10:7). Some legacies are blessings; others we would rather forget.

Paul's legacy was clearly on his mind when he wrote his second letter to Timothy: "I am now ready to be offered, and the time of my departure is at hand" (2 Timothy 4:6). He was aware that the picture he had been painting with his life was nearly complete, and he was confident that, by God's grace, it was something good: "I have fought a good fight, I have finished my course, I have kept the faith. Henceforth there is laid up for me a crown of righteousness, which the Lord, the righteous judge, shall give me on that day" (4:7-8).

Paul's legacy, and the legacies of his many companions and opponents, have something to teach us about the pictures we are painting on the canvases of our own lives.

Legacies of Harm and Help

Not all in the New Testament painted pictures like Paul's. As he reflected on his own legacy, he also had something to say about the people who labored with him— and those who did not.

In 2 Timothy's first chapter, Paul records the names of Phygellus and Hermogenes to mark how they deserted him. In fact, they were the exemplars of "all who are in Asia"—that is, Anatolia, or modern Turkey—who he says, "turned away from me" (1:15). Then there is Demas, who, "in love with this present world, has deserted me" (4:10). These names have gone down in the pages of biblical history as belonging to those who were unfaithful to a needful brother.

Some people not only fail to do good but also actively do evil. Such were "Hymenaeus and Philetus," who Paul describes as having "swerved from the truth" and who taught their false doctrine to others so that it spread around "like gangrene" (2 Tim. 2:17-18), and "Alexander the coppersmith," who did Paul "great harm" (4:14). Theirs are toxic legacies—memories that will rot.

But some brothers and sisters in Christ left legacies of significant help. Paul names Timothy's mother and grandmother, Lois and Eunice, as godly influences in Timothy's life. It was they who ensured that Timothy was "acquainted with the sacred writings" from childhood (2 Timothy 3:15). And Paul praises Mark as "very useful to me for ministry," and Tychicus as well (4:11–12). All of these preached the truth faithfully and advanced the course of the Gospel. And what a legacy has been left by Onesiphorus, about whom Paul wrote, "He often refreshed me and was not ashamed of my chains, but when he arrived in Rome, he searched for me earnestly and found me" (1:16–17). And Luke, too, remained with Paul (4:11). Each of these people was faithful to Paul when so many others deserted him.

These are significant legacies—both the good and the bad—recorded in Scripture to warn us and encourage us. And this is just a sampling of individuals connected to Paul. There are countless other examples for us to consider throughout Scripture. And when we give them consideration, they confront us with a question.

What About Us?

If you died tomorrow, what kind of legacy would you leave behind? One of the reasons that we want to steel ourselves against the prospect of death is that most of us do not want to think seriously about such a weighty topic. But if we are to leave a legacy of help and not of harm, we need to take seriously what kind of portrait we are painting right now.

The psalmist prays, "Teach us to number our days that we may apply our hearts unto wisdom" (Psalms 90:12). When we number our days, pray for wisdom, and resolve to live in the ways listed above, we can hope for a legacy that will bless, strengthen, and help those who come after us—not for our renown but for God's glory alone.

What is the Meaning and Origin of the Legacy of Truth?

1. The gospel is a divine plan. "Christ died for our sins in accordance with the Scriptures," which were written hundreds of years before Christ died (1 Corinthians 15:3). This means God had a plan, and if He did not, we have no gospel — it was just a fluke of history. But it is all written down in the Old Testament, hundreds of years before it happened, and Paul says

that is essential. Scripture was written by prophets who through the guidance of the Holy Spirit penned the words written.

2. The gospel is not only a plan of God, it is a historical event. Christ died. Christ rose again. If that did not happen historically, so that you can see it with your physical eyes, we have no gospel. A lot of modern people try to discredit this and just turn it into ideas. It is not an idea. Jesus ate fish after the Resurrection.

3. The gospel is a divine achievement through that event of suffering and resurrection. By achievement, I mean things like He died for our sins, which we see at the end of verse 3. Christ died for our sins.

   There is a design in it. There is an accomplishment. Something is achieved in this death. It is not a random death. God has a design. He is accomplishing something through the historical event like:

   - covering our sins (Colossians 2:14).

   - removing God's wrath (Romans 8:3)

   - and purchasing eternal life (John 3:16)

4. These are objective achievements of an objective event, which are true whether you come into existence two

thousand years later or not. This means that salvation is a gift. It is out there to accept His will and embrace the truth. God did it in history. It is there, it is done, and then I am born two thousand years later. Jesus cried out from the cross "It is finished" as He died for the sins of the entire world.

5. The gospel is a free offer of Christ for faith, not works. Christ is offered to you for faith alone. "The gospel I preached to you, which you received, in which you stand, and by which you are being saved, if you hold fast to the word I preached to you — unless you believed in vain" (1 Corinthians 15: 1-2). Note the two words receive and believe, just like in John 1:12). "But to all who did receive him, who believed in his name, he gave the right to become children of God." That is what it is to receive the gospel. You cannot work for this. It is based on Christ alone. It is external, outside of you — achieved and accomplished two thousand years ago. Now you are born. You hear that news. What do you do? I am going to start working for God so I can impress Him with how morally worthy I am. You are not, and you never get there that way. You receive it. You believe it. You embrace Jesus as your Treasure and your Lord and your Savior from all that you need saving from, and you are then saved forever. It is an awesome gospel. The gospel is an application of the

achievements accomplished in history to your heart when you believe. Forgiveness of sins was purchased once and applied now. All your sins are forgiven when you believe. Justification: You were not justified when Jesus died. You are justified when you believe, when it becomes yours. Then the purchase of the justification and the performance of the righteousness two thousand years ago is applied. That is why I am using the word application. It is applied to you. Eternal life: You did not have eternal life when Jesus died. You have eternal life when you believe. And then what He bought out there, what He wrought out there, becomes yours through the connection with Jesus through faith. So, the gospel is the application to believers of all that He purchased and achieved two thousand years ago.

6. The gospel is the enjoyment of fellowship with God Himself. Now if you ask, "Where do you see that?" Well, I see it outside (1 Corinthians 15: 1-3), but where I see it inside this text is in the word gospel. Gospel means good news, right? So, you must ask what is good about the good news? And if you stop after "My sins are forgiven" or "I'm vindicated in the court and can go free and I have life forever," and do not even mention God, that is serious. Simply put, God's plan of salvation is the divine romance recorded in the pages of the Bible. Biblical salvation is God's way

of providing His people deliverance from sin and spiritual death through repentance and faith in Jesus Christ.

John 8:32-33 states, "…and ye shall know the truth, and the truth shall make you free. They answered him, we be Abraham's seed, and were never in bondage to any man: how sayest thou, Ye shall be made free? Jesus answered them, Verily, verily, I say unto you, whosoever committeth sin is the servant of sin."

Chapter Nineteen

Truth Revealed

When any person speaks of truth, or about truth, it is interpreted differently among the brethren, according to morals and values and biblical ethics. When Jesus speaks, He is the way, the truth, and the life. He starts with the truth and ends with the truth. He cannot lie. His promises are true, His mercies are new every morning, and His words are everlasting.

Whatever stage of life we are in, we need to trust and obey His holy Word. As time marches on there are more signs that His second coming is near. We will now research what God's Word says about this monumental event.

The second coming of Jesus has been prophesied for years; it is completely foundational to the Gospel, which matters not only to the birth, death, resurrection, and the ascension of God the Son, but also His return for His bride. This event and the doctrines that surround it are integral to the "faith that was once for all delivered to the saints" (Jude 3).

*Four Assurances Concerning the Second Coming of
Christ Jesus.*

1. No man knows the day (the day is secret).

First and foremost, the day has not been disclosed in this
dispensation of grace. It is secret and will be revealed until the
Parousia-Christ's reappearing. Mark 13:32 states, "But of that
day and that hour, knoweth no man, no, not the angels which
are in heaven, neither the Son, but the father."

2. His return will be sudden.

His return will come as a thief in the night (Matthew
24:42-44); it will be quick. Second, the return of Jesus Christ
will be sudden. Just as lightning blazes across the sky this
event will happen quickly, and those who are in Christ will be
changed in the twinkling of an eye (Matthew 24:27).

The key text for the sudden nature of Christ's appearance
comes from Acts 1:11. After Christ's ascension to heaven,
angels appeared to the dazed disciples and asked, "Men of
Galilee, why do you stand looking up to heaven? This Jesus
who was taken up from you into heaven, will come in the
same way as you saw Him go into heaven."

Christ will return bodily, visibly, and suddenly. Just as He
went into heaven, so will He in like manner return to Earth.

It will be like a typical day, just another day at the office, just another day in the fields. People will be giving birth, dropping their children off at school, and other events will be happening, all in the same way as the day before. (Matthew 24:37-41). And there will be no tomorrow, for the former things that have passed away.

3. The event will be spectacular.

Christ's second coming will be remarkably different from His first. The shepherds followed a star and would seek out the Son in the manger (Luke 2: 15-16), and the three Wise Men had to inquire with King Herod in Jerusalem (Matthew 2: 1-2). Christ's second coming will not be like that at all. It will be startling and spectacular when He returns for His bride.

The Lord Himself will descend from heaven with a cry of command, with the voice of an archangel, and with the sound of a trumpet of God (1 Thessalonians 4:16). Jesus' return will prove unmistakable, as it bends and breaks the limits of space and time as we know them. We cannot predict the hour in which this will occur, but surely no creature will be left unaware when the Lord of Lords and the King of Kings returns to rescue His people and conquer the rebellious (Revelation 17:14).

4. His return will bring separation.

Finally, Christ will return in judgment to judge the living and the dead. Christ's inaugural mission was not to condemn but to save (John 3:17). When He returns, however, He will separate the faithful from the rebellious (Matthew 24: 38-41). Christ's sheep will inherit the kingdom prepared for them from the foundation of the world (Matthew 25: 34-40), but those who did not love Christ and are not saved as our Lord prescribed will depart into the fires of eternal punishment. (Matthew 25: 41-46).

Implications of Christ's Imminent Return.

While these four truths are certain, they are not simply ideas to ponder. The prospect of our Lord's imminent return should change how we live our lives now; it should affect us today, knowing that the time is growing nearer to the day of His return. We should be proclaiming the truth to our loved ones and all others. The Apostle John makes this plain for us.

"Beloved, we are God's children now, and what we will have has not yet appeared; but we know that when he appears we shall be like Him, because we shall see Him as He is. And everyone who thus hopes in Him purifies himself as He is pure" (I John 3:2-3).

We are not yet perfect, as is our destiny, but anyone who tethers their hope to heaven will come to know the kingdom's purifying effects. In other words, a person who professes

Christ and believes in His coming will increasingly align their life with the Lord's.

As it changes how we live, the second coming also promotes urgency in our evangelism. When Christ returns in power, it is glorious indeed, but will prove to be terrible for those who do not know Him as their savior. Share with others the everlasting life and joy found only in Him.

One Final Word.

The apostles seemed to speak as if Parousia was near, yet two thousand years removed from the events and writings of the New Testament, we still await this great and notable day when Jesus returns. When we are tempted to grow impatient and weary, we need to remember this especially important truth: with the Lord one day is as a thousand years, and a thousand years as one day. "The Lord is not slow to fulfill His promise as some count slowness, but is patient toward you, not wishing that any should perish, but that all should reach repentance" (2 Peter 3: 8-9).

Our sovereign God stands outside of time. The span of two millennia, let alone eternity, is inconceivable to our finite minds. His ways are higher than our ways. God has laid out a timeline of events that must be fulfilled according to His Word. Remember, when impatience wells up within us, we need to remind ourselves that God, in His inexhaustible providence and compassion, is supremely patient, more than we deserve. Christ Himself has testified,

"Surely I am coming soon." And all God's people respond, "Amen. Come, Lord Jesus!" (Revelation 22:20).

Jesus' Warnings and Promises of the Second Coming.

Jesus Christ unveils His warnings, reprimands, and promises to believers who overcome in those first century churches as well as today. (Revelation 1-3).

- Overcomers will eat of the tree of life in the paradise of God.

- Overcomers will not be hurt by the second death.

- Overcomers will receive hidden manna, a white stone with a new name.

- Overcomers will have authority over the nations as Jesus rules with a rod of iron and they will receive the morning star.

- Overcomers will be clothed in white garments and their names will not be removed from the book of life and Jesus will confess their names before the Father and His angels.

- Overcomers will become pillars in the temple of the Lord God and will have God's name and the name of God's city, and Jesus' new name on them.

- Overcomers will sit down with Jesus on the throne.

The angel instructed John to write the things which he saw, the things which are, and the things which will take place after these things. "Blessed is he who reads, and those who hear the words of the prophecy, and heed the things which are written in it; for the time is near" (Revelations 1:3).

Events to take place before the second coming of Christ. What comes first? Apostasis.

In Revelation 4 through 22, Jesus shows John what takes place after these things (John 13:19). Overcomers, believers, the church, are commanded to carry the gospel message until God says to His Son, "Go get my children." In 2 Thessalonians 2:3, the Bible states, "Let no one in any way deceive you by any means, for that day will not come unless the falling away comes first, and the man of sin is revealed, the son of perdition."

The falling away and the man of sin: falling away comes from the Greek word "Apostasis," deflection from truth, revolt, apostasy. The next Greek word describes the son of perdition; "Apoleia," ruin, loss, destruction, damnable. He is a man of lawlessness. Those who search the scriptures will know him by his actions. God's Word says there will be no question of his identity when he appears.

The Seven Seals as Judgements.

The events of the Bible identified in Revelation chapter 6 take John to the throne of God, where Jesus is holding a book that is sealed. Jesus breaks the first of seven sealed judgements on the earth. The first four are known as the Four Horsemen who are assigned different judgements and destructions carried out to portions of the earth; and while we know the events are sequential, we do not know the time frame between these judgements.

The First Horseman (white horse) goes out to conquer. The second one (a fiery red horse) goes out and is instructed to take peace from the earth. The Third Horseman (black horse) goes out, holding a pair of weighing scales in his hand. (Possibly regarding the collapse of world leadership and famine leading to a world-wide political catastrophe and a global government becoming reality?) Revelation 6:8, "And I looked and behold a pale horse: and his name that sat on him was Death, and Hell followed with him. And power was given unto them over the fourth part of the earth, to kill with sword, and with hunger, and with death, and with the beasts of the earth." A covenant with Israel and the building of the

Jewish Tribulation Temple? These are all events that signal the beginning of Daniel's 70th week. Daniel 9:24-27 is a detailed and complex prophecy that accurately dates the first coming of the Messiah, Jesus Christ, and discusses the establishing of the New Covenant and implications of events that will occur leading up to the time of Christ's second coming. "Seventy weeks are determined for your people and for your holy city, to finish the transgression, to make an end of sins, to make reconciliation for inquiry, to bring in everlasting righteousness, to seal up vision and prophecy, and to anoint the most Holy. Know therefore and understand, that from the going forth of the command to restore and build Jerusalem until Messiah the Prince, there shall be seven weeks and sixty-two weeks: the streets shall be built again, and the wall, even in troublesome times. And after the sixty-two weeks Messiah shall be cut off, but not for Himself; and the people of the prince who is to come shall destroy the city and the sanctuary. The end of it shall be with a flood, and till the end of war desolations are determined. Then he shall confirm a covenant with many for one week; but in the middle of the week, He shall bring an end to sacrifice and offering. And on the wing of abominations shall be one who makes desolate, even until the consummation, which is determined, is poured out on the desolate." Verse 24 lists six things that are to be accomplished by the end of the 70 weeks of Daniel: (1) Finish the transgression (2) Make an end of sins (3) Make reconciliation (atonement) for iniquity

(4) Bring in everlasting righteousness (5) Seal up vision and prophecy and (6) Anoint the "Most Holy." The scripture indicates that there will be three-plus years of relative peace, while the Jews are allowed to begin their sacrificial system.

The three final seals usher in more catastrophic judgements and scenes, ending with events that God's Word says must take place before the second return of Christ Jesus. The sixth seal will bring an earthquake, the sun will become black, the moon becomes like blood, and the stars of the sky fall to earth. The sky will be split apart like a scroll and men will hide from the mighty wrath of God.

Two Witnesses Proclaim the Gospel.

The book of Revelation proclaims what will happen as the two witnesses proclaim the gospel. In Revelation 11:3-5 reads, "And I will give power to my two witnesses, and they will prophesy a thousand two hundred and threescore days, clothed in sackcloth. These are the two olive trees and the two candlesticks standing before the God of the earth. And if man will hurt them, fire proceedeth out of their mouth and devoureth their enemies: and if any man will hurt them, he must in this manner be killed." While there is considerable speculation and controversy over who the two men are, some people believe one of them will be Elijah. Malachi 4:5-6 reads, "Behold, I will send you Elijah the prophet before the coming of the great and dreadful day of the Lord: And he shall turn the heart of the fathers to the children, and the heart of the children to their fathers, lest I come and smite the earth with a curse." Revelation 11: 9-10 states, "And they of the people and kindreds and tongues and nations shall see their dead bodies three days and an half, and shall not suffer their dead bodies to be put into graves, And they that dwell upon the earth shall rejoice over them, and make merry, and shall send gifts one to another; because these two prophets tormented them that dwelt on the earth."

No one can harm these two witnesses for three and one-half years as they preach the truth of the gospel. Can you imagine the propaganda press media coverage? Technology would allow this event to be seen in real-time, world-wide, in the comfort of your home.

Between the sixth and seventh trumpets this anti-Christ will kill these two witnesses. They will lay dead in the streets of Jerusalem for three and a half days while people celebrate their death. But God will then say, "Come up here." And they will ascend into heaven in a cloud.

Meanwhile, ten kings are ruling the world. One of these ten, the little-horn or anti-Christ, gains greater power, and will eliminate three of these kings.

The Trumpet Judgements.

Revelation 8:1-3 reads, "And when he had opened the seventh seal, there was silence in heaven for about the space of half an hour. And I saw the seven angels which stood before God; and to them were given seven trumpets. And another angel came and stood at the altar, having a golden censer; and there was given unto him much incense, that he should offer it with the prayers of all saints upon the golden altar which was before the throne."

Centuries ago, King David confirmed that God saves our prayers and our tears. As these trumpet judgements unfold, another necessary thing that must take place before the second coming of Christ is that hail, fire, and smoke mixed with blood will be cast from heaven to earth. The first trumpet fulfills this prophecy. Each of the trumpets increase in intensity. God sends three woes on those dwelling on earth to accompany the remaining trumpets. Between the sixth and seventh trumpet judgements, the scene abruptly changes, as do the attitudes of people who manage to survive. In Revelation, we are told of this leader, this beast who is killed by a fatal head wound then healed. He goes into the Jewish Temple, proclaims that he is God, breaks his covenant, and makes war with Israel. God gives him the authority to act for forty-two months. And anti-Christ's false prophets will then set up a cashless society in which you must take a mark on your hand or in your forehead to be able to buy or sell. This mark is the number 666, "the mark of the beast." Those who refuse this mark will be beheaded in this world, but those who take the mark of the beast will never inherit the kingdom of God: they will spend eternity with Satan in the lake of fire. Revelation 13:16-17 says, "And he causeth all, both small and great, rich, and poor, free and bond, to receive a mark in their right hand, or in their foreheads: And that no man might buy or sell, save he that had the mark, or the name of the beast or the number of his name." Revelation 13:18 reads, "Here is wisdom, let him that hath understanding count the number of the beast; for it is the number of a man; and his number is six hundred threescore and six."

God Does Not Forget His People.

Paul exclaims in the book of Romans chapter 11:2-5, "God hath not cast away his people which he foreknew. Wot ye not what the scripture saith of Elias? How he maketh intercession to God against Israel saying, Lord, they have killed the prophets, and dug down thine altars; and I am left alone, and they seek my life. But what saith the answer of God unto him? I have reserved to myself seven thousand men, who have not bowed the knee to the image of Baal. Even so then at this present time also there is a remnant according to the election of grace."

God's covenant with Israel is conclusive. God does not or cannot lie. God will prepare a place in the wilderness of Petra (where many believe that God is sheltering the remnant of His people) for the remnant of the Jewish people, hidden where they will be encamped in safety for three and a half years, where they will come to know Jesus as their Messiah and King.

Meanwhile, God has prepared seven final bowls of His wrath to be poured out upon the earth. Revelation 16:1 reads, "And I heard a great voice out of the temple saying to the seven angels, go your ways, and pour out the vials of the wrath of God upon the earth." Each bowl poured out brings greater destruction upon the wicked. The Word tells us that with each bowl those alive did not repent of their deeds. The last and final bowl, the greatest earthquake ever, splits Jerusalem into three parts, cities of the nations fall, huge hailstones about one hundred pounds each come down from heaven upon men, and they still blaspheme God. These extremely perverse people seal their doom.

Romans 11:25-27 says, "For I would not, brethren, that ye should be ignorant of this mystery, lest ye should be wise in your own conceits; that blindness in part is happened to Israel, until the fullness of the gentiles come in. And so, all Israel shall be saved: as it is written, there shall come out of Sion the Deliverer, and shall turn away ungodliness from

Jacob: For this is my covenant unto them, when I shall take away their sins."

The King is Coming.

Islands and mountains have fled away. Satan and his two beasts have lured the armies of the world to three battle scenes. One is in Babylon where Satan's armies, prompted by God, destroy Babylon. Then Satan and his armies invade Jerusalem and plunder the city and violate and kill the people. Thinking he (Satan) is victorious, he and his armies run towards the wilderness, and get as far as the Valley of Jehoshaphat. In that moment, the heavens open, and behold a white horse, and He who sat on it is called Faithful and True, and in His righteousness He judges and wages war, and the armies which are in heaven clothed in fine linen, white and clean were following Him on white horses. From His mouth comes a sharp sword, so that with it He may strike down the nations and He will rule them with a rod of iron. And on His robe and on His thigh, He has a name written, "KING OF KINGS, AND LORD OF LORDS." Think of this very glorious scene when the heavens open and King Jesus appears followed by all who have believed and trusted in His name and their names are written in the Lamb's book of life.

Just remember, "It could happen in a moment, in the twinkling of an eye," Jesus could return and split the eastern sky. Will you be ready for His appearance?

Revelation 14:20, "And the winepress was trodden without the city, and the blood came out of the winepress, even unto the horse bridles, by the space of a thousand and six hundred furlongs."

Chapter Twenty

"Grace Wins"

Now that we have examined God's timeline of events, we will examine what grace represents. When you hear the word "grace," what does that mean to you? Do you think of "Amazing grace, how sweet the sound, which saved a wretch like me, I once was lost, but now I am found, was blind, but now I see?" I have heard that song since childhood, and I am a firm believer that the person who wrote that song realized one thing: we are sinners saved by grace. Without Jesus, our hope of glory, we are lost and undone, wretched, poor, and naked, still under the bondage of sin, bound for an eternity in hell. The word "grace" is defined as an unmerited favor of God toward man. The Bible tells us that God's grace is manifested in the person of Jesus Christ. John 1:14 , "And the word was made flesh and dwelt among us, (and we beheld his glory, the glory as of the only begotten of the father,) full of grace and truth." John 1:16 says, out of his fullness we have all received grace in a place of grace already given. In other words, grace upon grace. The word became flesh and made His dwelling among us. We have seen His glory, the glory of the one and only Son, who came from the Father, full of grace and truth. Out of His fullness we have all received grace in place of grace already given.

John 1:14-17 states, "and the Word was made flesh and dwelt among us, and we beheld His glory, the glory as of the only begotten of the Father, full of grace and truth. John bare witness of Him and cried, saying 'This was He of whom I spoke, He that cometh after me is preferred before me: For He was before me. And of His fullness have all we received, and grace for grace. For the law was given by Moses, but grace and truth came by Jesus Christ.'"

The word "grace" appears in the Old Testament around sixty times. The theological concept of importance to us is the grace of God demonstrated toward man. The term occurs most often in the phrase "favor in your sight" or "in the eyes of the Lord." This assumes the notion of God as a watchful Master or King, with the one who is finding favor being a servant, an employee, or a soldier. In Genesis 6:8, the first concept appears as Noah finds grace in the eyes of the Lord. The context is that the Lord was grieved at how great man's wickedness on the Earth had become (Genesis 6:5). This statement about the Lord's dislike toward man's behavior is followed by His promise that He will wipe humankind from the face of the Earth and destroy him, because of His anger at their condition. Now, what is then described as having found favor in the eyes of the Lord and followed him in obedience? Judgment and salvation, and which most of the humankind are condemned to destruction, while God finds favor on a few (Noah and his family), reoccurs often in connection with the idea of grace. Hence, concepts of election, salvation, mercy, and forgiveness are all linked in this illustration of grace and the Old Testament.

In Exodus thirty-three is recorded the conversation between God and Moses, and in the space of six verses Moses is found to have said that he has found favor with God or God has been pleased with him five times. At the beginning of the chapter, Moses goes into the tent for a meeting, while the pillar of cloud stands at the entrance to the tent, and the people of Israel stay outside, worshiping. The Lord speaks to Moses face to face, as a man speaks with his friend. In the passage, the conversation between Moses and the Lord must specifically carry out the favor that God shows Moses, and Moses requests that God demonstrate the favor toward him. Moses begins by reminding God that He has called Moses to lead these people, but that God has not let him know whom He will send with Moses. A statement echoes the original conversation between Moses and God at the Burning Bush in chapter three where God promises to send Aaron with Moses to help him to get the people out of Egypt. Here, the Lord promises only that His presence will go with Moses, and that He will give him rest. Moses has just stated that he knows

God's name and that he has found favor with God; he requests that God teach him His ways so that he may know Him and continue to find favor with Him. Moses demonstrates his humble dependence upon the grace of God by affirming that if God's presence does not go up with him, he does not want to be sent, because he knows that he will fail. But then he asked the reasonable question, "How will anyone know that You're pleased with me and with Your people unless You go with us?" God promises to go with Moses because God states, "I am pleased with you, and I know you by name." Moses then makes one of the most remarkable requests of God ever made in scripture, asking God to "show me your glory." Just as remarkable is that God answers his request positively. He promised to cause all His goodness to pass in front of Moses and that He will proclaim His name, Yahweh, in Moses' presence. He then makes a statement that is related to grace throughout scripture, one that Paul will quote in the context of election in Romans 9:15. "For he saith to Moses, 'I will have mercy on whom I will have mercy and I will have compassion on whom I will have compassion.'" This is a remarkable example of the unconditional and full character of the grace of God. God holds little back, only telling Moses that he "cannot see my face, for no one may see me and live." Even this is an act of unconditional love and full grace in that God has withheld from Moses what would destroy him. The passage closes with a strange instruction that God will cause His "glory" to pass by, with Moses being hidden in a cleft in a rock and covered with the hand of God until the glory has passed by. Then God will remove His hand and allow Moses to see the back of His glory, but not His face. Again, this protective, gracious act of God emphasizes the extent to which God is willing to go with His faithful servant to show His favor toward him.

In Numbers 11:4 through 17, Many people of Israel were complaining of having manna and not any meat to eat, Moses cries out unto the Lord in an apparently sincere state of vexation at the burden of judging this entire people by himself. "Moses replied: "I cannot carry all these people by myself; the burden is too heavy for me. Moses replied unto the Lord, "If this is how you're going to treat me, Put me to death right now. If I have found favor in your eyes and do not let me face my own ruin." God immediately gives Moses a solution to his problem by appointing 70 of the elders of Israel to help him carry the burden of the people, so that he will not have to carry it alone. The fact that the Lord brings judgment upon the people, however, does not violate the point of God's favor towards Moses in this passage. He still acts as a sovereign God who gives complete, merited favor to his servant Moses.

Another man of the Bible who finds favor in the eyes of the Lord is Samuel. In 1 Samuel 2:26, the boy Samuel is described as growing in stature and favor, not only with the Lord, but also with men. It is significant because it is a description of the growth of a child in the favor of God. Because he is merely a child, he cannot earn favor. Thus, God's grace toward those whom He loves grows in His extensiveness, as the child grows. This is perhaps no less important because of Samuel's unique relationship and salvation history. He is the last of the judges and is the transitional figure between the period of the judges and the period of the kings in Israel's history, as John the Baptist is in the New Testament between the Old Testament prophets and the New Testament evangelists.

In the life of David, we see him first as a young child tending sheep on the hillside, going on to defeat Goliath the giant with five smooth stones, to becoming king of Israel. David, from his youth to manhood, loved the Lord his God. According to First Samuel, David was the youngest son of Jesse, a man of Bethlehem, and served as a shepherd for his father before beginning his career as an aide at the court of Saul, Israel's first king. When Israel came into conflict with the Philistines, a people from a neighboring region, David's brothers went to fight for King Saul. Young David would travel back and forth to the camp to bring his brothers food and supplies. According to First Samuel 17, Goliath, a philistine giant who was heavily armed, challenged Saul for 40 days to send the man out to fight him. No one would face this warrior until David, armed only with a sling and stones, volunteered to defeat the giant. David hit the giant in the forehead, killing him. The Philistines, seeing their champion killed, lost heart and were easily put to flight. David continued being a warrior in the ongoing battles against the Philistines, and his popularity aroused Saul's jealousy. Fearing that the people would make David king, Saul plotted to have him killed. With the help of his loyal friend Jonathan, Saul's elder son, David fled into southern Judah and the coastal plains of Palestine, where with great wisdom and foresight, he began to lay the foundations of his career. In 1 Samuel 16, the boy David was anointed by the prophet Samuel as a future king of Israel; his actions in exile helped ensure that he would be invited to become king as a true successor after Saul and Jonathan were slain in a battle against the Philistines on Mount Gilboa. During David's kingship, he made a covenant with the elders of northern Israel and was anointed as king over all of Israel. David continued to be a great warrior. Here are a few passages of scripture which David wrote or is mentioned:

- Psalm 23:1 The Lord is my shepherd; I shall not want.

- 1 Chronicles 18:14 So David reigned over all Israel, and he administered justice and equity to all his people.

- Ezekiel 34:23 And I will set up over them one shepherd, my servant David, and he shall feed them: he shall feed them and be their shepherd.

- Psalm 144:1 (A Psalm of David) Blessed be the Lord my strength, which teacheth my hands to war, and my fingers to fight.

- Psalm 35:1-3 – (A Psalm of David) Contend, O Lord, with those who contend with me; fight against those who fight against me! Take hold of the shield and buckler and rise for my help! Draw the spear and javelin against my pursuers! Say to my soul, "I am your salvation!"

Another prominent example of grace in the Old Testament is found in the book of Esther. This book speaks of Esther's humility in seeking the favor of the king and points toward human responsibility to humbly accept the grace of God. Esther finds favor in the eyes of the king and is rewarded with the freedom of her people.

- Esther 1:17-18: The king loved Esther more than all the women, and she found favor and kindness with him more than all the virgins, so that he set the royal turban on her head and made her queen in place of Vashti. Then the king held a great banquet, Esther's banquet, for all his officials and his servants; he also made a holiday for the provinces and gave gifts in proportion to the king's bounty.

- Esther 4:14: "For if thou altogether holdest thy peace at this time, then shall their enlargement and deliverance arise to the Jews from another place; but thou and thy father's house shall be destroyed: and who knoweth whether thou art come to the kingdom for such a time as this?"

- Esther 4:16: "Go, gather together all the Jews that are present in Shushan, and fast ye for me."

Now we will examine what each chapter represents, and end with the marriage supper of the Lamb. As we look at the shape of society and where it is heading, we can only imagine what glory awaits the believer when Jeus returns for His bride. We have seen what happens when we walk not in truth and obedience.

The first chapter, "In God We Trust: Sands of Time," is a representation of the sands running out in the hourglass of our lives. Each person is given a "will" to follow Jesus or remain in their sin and follow the world. The past few years have taught us that we have no control when things happen to us; when we face trials and tribulations, we are nearer to eternity. As time marches on and world events unfold, we are listening for the sound of the trumpet. Just remember, "It could happen in a moment." (Are you ready?)

The second chapter represents the "United States (Richest Nation)." Can you see our God- given liberties disappearing? Can you look through your spiritual lenses and see all that is happening to our world? All sorts of chaos are happening (for sin and destruction have taken their stand). There are many false prophets that are teaching different doctrines rather than the truth. Make sure you are praying for our country and our world. (Pray for the peace of Israel.)

In chapter three, we look at the year "2020 Perfect Vision" and realize all the changes that have taken place since covid-19 (coronavirus) made its entrance into our once-safe world. Some companies may never recover the loss that happened, and the revenues lost to covid were astronomical.

Chapter four continues to expand on "An Invisible Enemy" (pandemic). This chapter dives deeper into the chaos and reminds us of the lessons we have learned through this experience.

Chapter five is a representation of what has happened in "Winds of Change: One Voice." Things have drastically changed. No matter how I vote, no matter what I say, something evil has invaded our nation, and our lives will never be the same. People are politically and religiously divided. Hostility and entitlement are the ways of the world. We need Jesus to make positive change in our nation and get back to being "One Nation under God."

Chapter six examines how we have always been united but are now divided by religion and politics. In all of history, there has never been more division between religion and politics. Our laws are constantly changing, our constitutional rights are being altered, and the biblical foundation on which America was founded is slowly diminishing right before our very eyes.

Chapter seven ushers in a new world order; in which things are continuing to become darker; evil is on the rise, and we are at the door of monumental change (not for the good). Things we have taken for granted all our lives, such as our God-given rights, liberties, and values, are quickly dispersing into evil hands.

Chapter eight examines a cashless society. Self-check outs and digital currency are only the beginning of what a cashless society will hold for our future. Every penny you receive will be recorded; every transaction will be tracked. There will be no buying anything with privacy; 100% digital currency means your life is 100% dependent on a power source and the internet.

Chapter nine explains war and rumors of war ("The War Still Rages"). In this chapter we look at how close we are to going to war. We are in a spiritual battle for good versus evil. The Bible gives examples of what that time will represent for those left behind in the Rapture. The final battle between God and Satan as described in the Bible is the battle of Armageddon. We examine the rise of the anti-Christ and his defeat.

Chapter ten examines the "Signs of the Times," things that are happening and have happened to set the stage for the end times. World catastrophic events, chaotic weather patterns, worldwide wildfires, etc. A falling away from the church, loss of our constitutional rights. People are at the forefront of trying to rewrite history. Immoral society allows wrong to become right (being right in their own eyes).

Chapter eleven describes the "Beginning of Sorrows (a Time of Jacob's Trouble)." How awful that day will be! It will be "the time of Jacob's trouble, Jacob being an advocate for all the nation of Israel." Jeremiah 30: 5-6: "For thus saith the Lord; We have heard a voice of trembling, of fear, and not of peace. Ask ye now, and see whether a man doth travail with child? Wherefore do I see every man with his hands on his loins, as a woman in travail, And all faces are turned into paleness?" Verse 5 describes Jacob's trouble as a time of great fear and trembling. Verse 6 describes it in terms of the pains of childbirth, indicating a time of agony. But there is hope for the people of Israel, for the Lord promises He will save them. Even though this is the time of Jacob's distress and even though "in all of history there has never been such a time of terror" God will deliver His people.

Chapter twelve examines "Will There Be Peace? (Israel Under Fire). (Israel has always been under attack; however, God has always saved them from destruction. God had chosen Israel for His treasured possession, out of all the peoples who are on the face of the earth. Deuteronomy 14:2, "For thou art an holy people unto the Lord thy God, and the Lord hath chosen thee to be a peculiar people unto himself, above all the nations that are upon the earth." We must get to know His beloved people for these five reasons: their interactions with God reveal his character. The Bible demonstrates and displays God's mercy. Righteousness, consistency, reliability, wrath, love, goodness, and His almighty power towards the nation of Israel.

Chapter thirteen represents "A Fallen Nation." What happened from our humble beginnings to where we are in this era? A nation that was founded on biblical principles and moral ethics has become decayed. Scriptures teach that God has a purpose, a divinely ordained role, for every nation. God will punish evil doers and protect the innocent. Romans 13:3-4, "For rulers are not a terror to good works, but to the evil."

Chapter fourteen is a plea: "America, Turn Back to God." The consequences of the wages of sin as spoken in the Bible are death. This represents the death of a nation and physical death. Eternal separation from our creator resulting in eternal damnation.

Chapter fifteen is a representation of the consequences of "God's Spirit Removed." Sin and destruction have set the stage as the end times draw nearer. The Bible clearly says to heed the warning. Christ will remove all born-again believers from the earth in an event known as the Rapture (see 1 Thessalonians 4:13-18; 1 Corinthians 15:51-54). At the judgment seat of Christ, these believers will be rewarded for good works and faithful service during their time on earth or will lose rewards, but not eternal life, for lack of service and obedience (1 Corinthians 3:11-15; 2 Corinthians 5:10). God's Word states in 2 Corinthians 5:10, "For we must all appear before the judgment seat of Christ; that everyone may receive the things done in his body, according to that he hath done, whether it be good or bad."

Chapter sixteen represents "America Judged (God's Wrath Revealed)." What happens when God reveals His wrath? The Bible states in Philippians 2:12-13, "Wherefore, my beloved, as ye have always obeyed, not as in my presence only, but now much more in my absence, work out your own salvation with fear and trembling. For it is God which worketh in you both to will and to do His good pleasure." God must act justly and judge sin, otherwise God would not be God.

Behold the vengeance of the Lord! Wrath has gone forth, a whirling tempest; it will burst upon the head of the wicked. Jeremiah 30:23 states, "Behold the whirlwind of the Lord goeth forth with fury, a continuing whirlwind: it shall fall with pain upon the head of the wicked." Nahum 1:2 says, "God is jealous, and the Lord revengeth; the Lord revengeth, and is furious; the Lord will take vengeance on his adversaries and he reserveth wrath for his enemies."

Romans 1:18 reads, "For the wrath of God is revealed from heaven against all ungodliness and unrighteousness of men, who hold the truth in unrighteousness."

Chapter seventeen is a beautiful picture of "God as the Alpha and Omega (The Beginning and End)." Just as the book of Ecclesiastes states that there is nothing new under the sun, all things were created by Him and for Him. Ecclesiastes 1: 9, "The thing that hath been, it is that which shall be and that which is done is that which shall be done: and there is no new thing under the sun." Ecclesiastes 3:2 states, "A time to be born, and a time to die; a time to plant, and a time to pluck up that which is planted." If we could have more time, what would we spend our time doing? Love more, serve more, tell more people about the plan of salvation, or would we wish for more time to do our earthly pleasures? (I wish I would have found Jesus sooner and loved Him longer).

Chapter eighteen ushers in "A Legacy of Truth." This chapter represents the absolute truth of salvation, examines the Word in our lives, expresses our need to live and walk in spirit and in truth. What will you be remembered for?

Did you use your time, talent, and testimony for the cause of Christ? It's not too late to start now. Grow in grace, live in His wonderful truth, and add to the kingdom. The psalmist prays, "Teach us to number our days that we may apply our hearts unto wisdom" (Psalms 90:12). When we number our days, pray for wisdom, and resolve to live in the ways listed above, we can hope for a legacy that will bless, strengthen, and help those who come after us, not for our renown but for God's glory alone.

Chapter nineteen represents "Truth Revealed." In this chapter we examine Jesus, "the way, the truth, and the life." We look at truths concerning the Second Coming of Christ. He is returning for His bride (the body that represents every born-again believer). Jesus gives warnings of His Second Coming and what to expect when this most important event takes place. After these things, the next and final event is the marriage supper of the Lamb. We read about this in the book of Revelation 19:7-10, "Let us be glad and rejoice and give honor to him: for the marriage of the lamb is come and his wife hath made herself ready. And to her was granted that she should be arrayed in fine linen, clean and white, for the fine linen is a righteousness of Saints. And he saith unto me, right blessed are they which are called unto the marriage supper on the lamb and he saith unto me these are the true sayings of God. And I fell at his feet to worship him, and he said unto me, see thou do it not; I am thy fellow servant and of thy brethren that have the testimony of Jesus: worship God for the testimony of Jesus is the spirit of prophecy." We see in verse seven the "marriage of the Lamb" take place, and in verse nine we read about the "marriage supper of the Lamb." In Bible times, the Jewish marriage customs consisted of both the "marriage" and "marriage supper." This Jewish custom included a great celebratory feast after the bride and groom were married. The marriage of Christ, the Lamb, to the church, His bride, will be a spectacular ceremony, only to be followed by the breathtaking wedding feast, the "marriage supper of the Lamb." This will take place after the church has been taken to heaven in the Rapture, and following the judgment seat of Christ, but it will happen before we return with Christ to Earth at His glorious appearance. This means the marriage of the Lamb and the marriage supper of the Lamb will take place in paradise, which is heaven. This incredible end time event will include the Bridegroom, who is the Lamb, Jesus Christ, and the bride, who is the church. Every person who is a member of the body of Christ will be there as the bride; as a believer you are cordially invited to the marriage supper of the Lamb. From the moment you accepted Jesus Christ as your Lord and Savior, you became part of the bride-to-be. This will be your wedding feast. The guests that will be invited to the marriage supper of the lamb are Old Testament saints such as Abraham, Isaac, and Jacob, Moses, Joshua, and David, who were all in heaven; however they are not part of the church, thus they are not the bride, they are "a great cloud of witnesses" as spoken in Hebrews 12:1. John the Baptist, one of the New Testament saints, identifies himself as a friend of the bridegroom. In John 3:29, "He that hath the bride is the bridegroom: but the friend of the bridegroom, which standeth and heareth him, rejoiceth greatly because of the bridegroom's voice: this my joy therefore is fulfilled." All the believing dead from Adam until the resurrection of Christ will be guests at this wedding feast. While we are celebrating this great feast in heaven, the angels of the Lord are carrying out God's judgements of the Great Tribulation here on earth.

Scriptures representing the "marriage supper of the Lamb."

Matthew 25: 1-5, "At that time the kingdom of heaven will be like ten virgins who took their lamps and went out to meet the bridegroom. Five of them were foolish and five of them were wise. The foolish ones took their lamps but did not take any oil with them. The wise ones, however, took oil in jars along with their lamps. The bridegroom was a long time in coming, and they became drowsy and fell asleep."

John 14:3, "And if I go and prepare a place for you, I will come again and receive you unto myself that where I am there ye may be also."

Revelation 3:20, "Behold I stand at the door, and knock if any man hears my voice, and open the door, I will come into him, and will sup with him, and he with me."

Scriptures preparing for the Lord's return.

I Thessalonians 4:16-17, "For the Lord himself shall descend from heaven with a shout, with the voice of the archangel, and with the trump of God and the dead in Christ shall rise first."

Titus 2:13, "Looking for that blessed hope and the glorious appearance of the Great God and our Savior Jesus Christ."

Hebrews 9:28, "So Christ was once offered to bear the sins of many; and unto them that look for him shall he appear the second time without sin unto salvation."

Revelation 1:7, "Behold he cometh with clouds and every eye shall see him and they also which pierced him, and all kinds of the earth shall wail because of him. Even so, Amen."

Revelation 21:1, "And I saw a new heaven and a new earth for the first heaven and the first earth were passed away and there was no more sea."

John 3:16 states, "For God so loved the world, that he gave his only begotten Son, that whosoever believeth in him should not perish, but have everlasting life."

Are you ready? Are your lamps trimmed and bright? Do you know the Bible says Jesus will come like a thief in the night? Are you washed by the blood of the Lamb? Is your name written in the Lamb's book of life? He's coming back to claim His bride. Make ready for His return and be saved before it is eternally too late.

Bibliography/References

Betley, Matthew. Rules of War. New York; Emily Bestler Books/Atria Books 2019.

"The Bible." The Bible. August 7, 2023. http://www.thebible.com.

Graham, Billy. The Holy Spirit September 27 http://billygraham.org/devotion/the-holy-spirit/

Christianity.com. What Do We Know About the Second Coming of Jesus

Bricker, Vivian. March 31, 2022. Christianity.com/wiki/end-times/what-do-we-know-about-the second-coming-of-Jesus-html.

CNN News. May 8, 2023, COVID-19 Pandemic Timeline Fast Facts. Accessed. May 12, 2023. CNN Editorial Research. Cnn.com/2021/08/09health/covid-19-pandemic-timeline-fast-facts/index.html

D'Souza, Dinesh. America. New York: Regnery Publishing A Salem Communications Company 2014.

FOX News. August 20, 2023, Danielle Wallace, Andrea Lacchiano. Accessed August 23, 2023.

In-text Citation:(FOX News)

Gulati, Ayush. Accessed August 4, 2023. Cashless Society: Pros and Cons of Embracing the Digital Dirham. http://www. cashlesssociety.org.

Bollinger, Hope. What and When Is the Battle of Armageddon? Accessed October 13, 2023. wiki/end-times/ what is http://www.the anti-Christ. christianity.com/ wiki/ end-times/what-is-the-battle-of-armageddon-meaning-significance.html

Piper, John. Will America Be Judged? February 25, 2014. http://www.desiringgod.org/articles/will-Americabe-judged?

August 12, 2023. http://www.kingjamesbibleonline. org./ search.php?hs=1&q=marriage+supper+of+the+lamb.

Nelson, Thomas. 2017. Deluxe Gift Bible, Red Letter Edition [Navy]. Thomas Nelson

Accessed October 12, 2023a. http://www.newworldorder. org.FourteenPoints-DigitalHistory https://www. digitalhistory. uh.edu

Accessed October 12, 2023e. http://www.thesignsofthe times.org.

The Fellowship. n.d. "News | International Fellowship of Christians and Jews." International Fellowship of

Christians and Jews. https://www.facebook.com/ FellowshipFan. , 2023. http://www.Israelunderfire.org.

August 20, 2023. Accessed. http://www.data.oecd. org/ united-states-.htm

Accessed August 22, 2023d. What Does The Bible Really Say about the Rapture?-ChristianitySeptember 15, 2022. http://www.the churchraptured.com

"World Health Organization (WHO)." n.d. World Health Organization (WHO). Accessed October 12, 2023. http:// www.WHO.org.

In-text Citation: ("World Health Organization (WHO)")

Related Sources

www.ingramcontent.com/pod-product-compliance
Lightning Source LLC
Chambersburg PA
CBHW060535160726
47991CB00001B/340